Lernthriller Englisch

KOMPLOTT UNTER PALMEN

Story: Susi Weichselbaumer
Übersetzung: Fiona Cain

Compact Verlag

Bisher sind in dieser Reihe erschienen:
- Compact Lernthriller Englisch Grammatik
- Compact Lernthriller Englisch Konversation
- Compact Lernthriller Englisch Grundwortschatz
- Compact Lernthriller Englisch Aufbauwortschatz

In der Reihe Lernkrimi sind erschienen:
- Compact Lernkrimi Englisch Grammatik
- Compact Lernkrimi Englisch Konversation
- Compact Lernkrimi Englisch Grundwortschatz
- Compact Lernkrimi Englisch Aufbauwortschatz
- Compact Lernkrimi Französisch Grundwortschatz
- Compact Lernkrimi Französisch Grammatik
- Compact Lernkrimi Italienisch Grundwortschatz
- Compact Lernkrimi Italienisch Grammatik
- Compact Lernkrimi Spanisch Grundwortschatz
- Compact Lernkrimi Spanisch Grammatik

Weitere Titel sind in Vorbereitung.

© 2004 Compact Verlag München
Alle Rechte vorbehalten. Nachdruck, auch auszugsweise,
nur mit ausdrücklicher Genehmigung des Verlages gestattet.
Chefredaktion: Evelyn Boos
Redaktion: Brigitte Stoffel
Fachredaktion: Karen Vaughan
Produktion: Wolfram Friedrich
Titelillustration: Karl Knospe
Typografischer Entwurf: Maria Seidel
Umschlaggestaltung: Carsten Abelbeck

ISBN 3-8174-7571-3
7275712

Besuchen Sie uns im Internet: www.compactverlag.de

Vorwort

Mit dem neuen, spannenden Compact Lernthriller können Sie Ihre Englischkenntnisse auf schnelle und einfache Weise vertiefen, auffrischen und überprüfen.

Agent Hunter erleichtert das Sprachtraining mit Action und Humor. Er und seine mysteriösen Fälle stehen im Mittelpunkt einer zusammenhängenden Story.

Der Thriller wird auf jeder Seite durch abwechslungsreiche und kurzweilige Übungen ergänzt, die das Lernen unterhaltsam und spannend machen.

Prüfen Sie Ihr Englisch in Lückentexten, Zuordnungs- und Übersetzungsaufgaben, in Buchstabenspielen und Kreuzworträtseln!

Ob im Bus oder in der Bahn, im Wartezimmer, zu Hause oder in der Mittagspause – das Sprachtraining im handlichen Format bietet die ideale Trainingsmöglichkeit für zwischendurch.

Schreiben Sie die Lösungen einfach ins Buch!

Die richtigen Antworten sind in einem eigenen Lösungsteil zusammengefasst.

Und nun kann die Spannung beginnen …

Viel Spaß und Erfolg!

Die Ereignisse und die handelnden Personen in diesem Buch sind frei erfunden. Etwaige Ähnlichkeiten mit tatsächlichen Ereignissen oder lebenden Personen wären rein zufällig und unbeabsichtigt.

Inhalt

Lernthriller 5
Abschlusstest 133
Lösungen 138

Story

Agent Peter Hunter ist ein alter Hase im Geschäft. Ob im In- oder Ausland, wann immer es gilt, das Verbrechen zu bekämpfen – Hunter ist zur Stelle und riskiert Leib und Leben. Unter seinen Kollegen beim Britischen Geheimdienst gilt er als Einzelgänger. Der Erfolg bei seinen Operationen gibt ihm Recht, auch wenn Hunter oft nur haarscharf dem Tod entrinnt.

Brennpunkt diesmal: eine kleine Inselgruppe im Pazifik. Umweltschützer protestieren gegen Atomtests. Die Demonstrationen werden gewaltsam von den Regierungsbehörden bekämpft. Und nicht nur von diesen. Was zunächst nach einem innenpolitischen Konflikt aussieht, entpuppt sich als weltweites Komplott. Wer steckt hinter den Waffentests auf den Inseln? Warum sterben die Bewohner? Welch grausame Funde muss Hunter bei seinen Ermittlungen vor Ort machen?
Sein junger, unerfahrener Assistent Percy Horn reist ihm auf eigene Faust nach ... Kann er helfen oder kommt seine Hilfe ohnehin zu spät? Hunter steht bereits zwischen den Fronten: Waffenschieber und Spitzenpolitiker. Und plötzlich wollen ihn alle aus dem Weg schaffen ...

Island intrigue

"Detonate!" thundered the Captain into the radio. There was strained silence on the bridge of the warship. The Captain held the radio to his mouth. It crackled and hissed. He stared through the wide window in front of him at the open sea. The first and second officers lined up behind him. They were all looking attentively towards him to see what would happen next.

Nothing happened. The Captain straightened. His dark-blue naval uniform sat perfectly. There was not a single hair out of place beneath his blue cap. He looked ahead defiantly. He waited a moment. "Will you detonate it, you fool!" he repeated. Some of the men who were lined up behind him jumped.

Übung 1: Unterstreichen Sie die Substantive im Text!

The Captain put down the radio. There was a smile on his face. On the small monitor in front of him, he followed the torpedo's progress through the water. He turned his gaze back to the window, looking for the orange buoy: the target of the torpedo exactly 50 metres ahead. The waves were not particularly high on this late afternoon, but he could not see the buoy. "Vargas! Binoculars!" he ordered.

A young man stepped obediently to his side. "Yes, Captain, Sir!" he said.
"Don't shout in my ear, Winston!" scolded the Captain. He took the binoculars from the officer, shouting, "Give them to me!" Vargas thought it was better not to reply. He bowed his head and stepped back. This mission was supposed to advance his position on the

career ladder. At least, that was what he wanted. But would he ever be recommended for a promotion by this Captain? Before he could think any more about this, the Captain's harsh voice rang out again. "Damnation, Lavalle! Let it off!"

"Captain? Now?" Lavalle asked hesitantly from behind his desk at the bridge.

"Now, or you'll be up before the military court for refusal to obey orders!" shouted the Captain. Lavalle pushed several switches. He was sweating. The torpedo was supposed to ignite itself on contact with the buoy. Why did the Captain want him to detonate it now, a good 200 metres before its proper target?

There was a dull thud through the window of the bridge. Then everything was quiet. There were dark-grey clouds in the air above the spot where the torpedo had exploded just below the surface of the water. The men on the bridge saw how the clouds slowly dissipated and disappeared.

Übung 2: Setzen Sie die Sätze ins Präsens!

1. The ship sailed into the harbour.

   The ship saile into the harbour

2. The Captain was angry.

   The Captain were angry

3. The soldier gave him the binoculars.

4. The man wore a dark-blue cap.

5. The Captain wanted to detonate the torpedo.

_____

6. The sailors saw the buoy in the distance.

_____

"Captain, Sir! Reporting! Fishing boat hit near the buoy!" said a voice from the radio. Slowly, the Captain lifted the radio to his lips. With his other hand, he absent-mindedly smoothed the uncreased surface of his uniform jacket. At the top of his voice, he thundered, "You idiot! You were responsible for hitting the target! You should report to me in advance if there is something in the test area! Not after the torpedo has been detonated!"

Noisy crackling came from the loudspeaker. It was impossible to understand what the other man was saying. "Get yourself up to the bridge!" thundered the Captain and switched off the radio. He hurled it onto the floor behind him. A few helpful officers tried to retrieve it. "Leave it, men," ordered the Captain gruffly.

Übung 3: Wie lauten die Infinitive der Verben?

1. fell   _____   6. shook   _____

2. said   _____   7. paid   _____

3. spoke   _____   8. told   _____

4. began _____   9. got   _____

5. sank   _____   10. held   _____

From the way the Captain was standing, it was obvious that he was thinking. He held his head to one side and looked at the blue waves. He lifted the binoculars to his eyes again. Once again, his tone was harsh as he ordered, "Vargas, take two men and get the speedboat ready. Go out to the fishermen over there. Make sure that there are no witnesses."

Vargas blinked under his cap. He did not fully understand and asked, "Sir, excuse me, Sir …."

The other man interrupted him sharply, "Then wear a gas mask, you wimp! Quick, march!"

Übung 4: Lesen Sie weiter und beantworten Sie folgende Fragen zum Text!

1. Who does Vargas bump into?

2. Why does Vargas nod his head?

3. What colour is the soldier's hat?

4. What does the soldier do that shows that he is nervous?

5. Is the soldier normally very strong or very weak?

At the door of the bridge, Vargas collided with a soldier who was running breathlessly along the passageway. The two men stood in each other's way for a moment. Then the soldier stepped back to allow his superior to exit. With a nod, Vargas thanked the man and left the room. The soldier, who was wearing a khaki uniform, was nervously twisting his dark-blue woollen hat in both hands. He was over six feet tall, his broad upper body was athletic and the muscles of his arms bulged underneath the tight material of his jacket. Normally strong and beefy, the man now looked weedy. His shoulders drooped, his head was bent and his eyes were fixed on the hat which he still held in his hands.

The Captain turned around. He stood with his back to the window. The evening sunlight was blood-red. The light shimmered on the brass instruments and controls. The polished dark wood of the wheel was a warm contrast to the metal.

*Übung 5: Setzen Sie **a, an** oder **some** ein!*

1. _____ order
2. _____ ship
3. _____ soldiers
4. _____ voice
5. _____ instruction
6. _____ radioactive matter
7. _____ obstruction
8. _____ time
9. _____ plan
10. _____ work

"Attention!" shouted the Captain of the ship to the soldier in front of him. The soldier straightened at the words. He stood upright but kept looking at the floor. The Captain went up to the man. The officers stepped backwards, forming a semi-circle. The soldier stood in the middle of the semi-circle. He did not move as the Captain walked around him in measured steps. The Captain's steel-blue eyes below his peaked cap scrutinised the younger man. There was silence.

"You will report in advance if there is something in the test area," began the Captain in a voice that was suddenly calm. He added, "Repeat." The soldier repeated what the Captain had said.

"You have ruined the whole test for us; I hope that's clear to you?" The Captain's voice was level. "Torpedo collides with buoy. Automatic detonation of the charge from the upper torpedo chamber without release of radioactive matter. That was the plan. Now what do we have, thanks to you?"

The soldier had stopped twisting his cap. He stood straight as a rod. He lifted his head as the other man resumed, "Sudden obstruction in the target area! We had to detonate prematurely! Now there's radioactive gas swirling around in the sky! Two fishermen without doubt not only witnessed the whole event but have also been totally exposed to radiation. Three of my best men are out there now getting rid of them!" As he spoke, the Captain prodded the soldier's broad chest with his index finger. The soldier looked at his superior squarely in the eye. He straightened again, pulling himself up to his full height. The Captain was half a head shorter than he was. Silently, the men stood facing each other for a moment.

Übung 6: Wie lautet der Plural der Substantive?

1. man _____   5. woman _____

2. sky _____   6. knife _____

3. child _____ 7. foot _____

4. country _____ 8. life _____

"Why didn't you just let the torpedo hit the boat? Then your three best men" – he emphasized these words – "wouldn't have had to go out and get rid of the fishermen. The fishermen would have been right at the source of the radiation and wouldn't have survived long. But now that they've been exposed to radiation …."

The Captain, looking up, was confused. Then he became angry. "Young man," he said, "are you by any chance questioning my orders?"

The soldier was now very angry also and dared to say, "Yes, Sir. That's what I'm doing." He blinked defiantly. He felt the officers' gaze on him. He, a soldier of low rank, was daring to say what they were all thinking. The soldier spoke again. "I *am* questioning your orders," he said proudly. "Do you want them to get rid of me now, too?"

The Captain's tone was condescending. He grasped underneath his uniform jacket as he spoke. "No, I'll look after you myself."

The force of the shot made the soldier topple backwards. He fell against the wheel and grabbed it with his hand. The wheel turned. The soldier lost his grip and fell to the floor. Blood streamed from the wound on his forehead.

His eyes clouded over. He stared at his comrades who stood around him. The Captain turned away.

Übung 7: Übersetzen Sie und unterstreichen Sie die Fragewörter!

1. Wo ist meine Kappe?

___

2. Wer war böse?

___

ÜBUNG 7

3. Was hat er dir gegeben?

4. Wann findet die Ausstellung statt?

5. Warum regnet es?

6. Wohin gehst du?

The muggy air hit Hunter as he left the airport building. He looked around for a taxi rank. There was a group of men loitering around several metres away. The men were talking animatedly. Many were smoking. They were leaning against small black cars. It seemed as though none of the taxi drivers wanted to stop chatting. In any case, no one took any notice of the new arrival. Hunter walked up to them and waited.

Suddenly, a young man in baggy jeans and a T-shirt hurried up to him. Without asking, he took Hunter's suitcase and indicated to the agent to follow him. The man led Hunter to the black taxi which stood at the end of the queue. "I hope that doesn't annoy any of the other drivers," thought Hunter. In London, you always had to take the first taxi in the queue, otherwise there was trouble. But he was not in England; he was on a small island in the middle of the Pacific Ocean.

"It's more casual here," decided the agent, as the young man threw his suitcase casually into the boot and shut the lid.

Übung 8: Setzen Sie die Verben im Text ins Simple Past!

The journey to the hotel (1. take) _____ a long time. The driver, who (2. have) _____ dreadlocks underneath his green, red and yellow knitted hat, (3. sing) _____ at the top of his voice to the music of Bob Marley on the car radio. At first, Hunter (4. speak) _____ to him, asking him questions about the country and its people. However, when the driver only (5. nod) _____ or (6. shake) _____ his head, Hunter (7. give up) _____ and (8. be) _____ silent.

They had been driving for over half an hour. The streets of the town were narrow and bumpy. The cobblestones were full of potholes. The rickety car jolted over the roads and its old engine droned loudly.
The taxi driver had probably driven around in a circle several times to increase the fare. Hunter thought he remembered many of the houses, but he did not mind. "The Secret Service will pay," he thought.
They arrived at the hotel. The fare was high. Once Hunter had paid, the car drove on. Thinking quickly, the agent banged his fist on the car roof and shouted, "Stop!"
The driver seemed reluctant as he stopped and climbed out of the car. He opened the boot. Impatiently, he indicated to Hunter to take his luggage out. Then the man with the dreadlocks raced off again. Disturbed, Hunter gazed after him for a few moments. "Other countries, other customs," he decided and entered the hotel.

Übung 9: Welches Wort im Text entspricht der Beschreibung?

1. Without much noise _____
2. Dirty or grubby _____
3. To walk lazily _____
4. The opposite of 'thin' _____
5. A room booking _____
6. To speak indistinctly _____
7. Counterfeit or fake _____

The revolving door squeaked quietly. The cramped reception area looked shabby. In the dim lamplight, a porter wearing a filthy uniform shuffled out of a back room. The fat man took up his position behind the desk and stared at the new arrival.

"Pieter Dyck from Amsterdam." Hunter introduced himself. "I made a reservation."

The porter mumbled something. He wrote a few words in a large book which lay open in front of him.

"That's a pity," thought Hunter. He had a forged identity card and had not even been asked for it.

Without requesting his passport or personal details, the man handed the key over the desk. Then he returned to the back room.

Übung 10: Verwenden Sie die richtige Form des Verbs *to be*!

The hotel porter (1.) _____ tired that evening. "I'm sorry, I (2.) _____ nearly asleep," he said to Hunter.

Hunter (3.) _____ not pleased. He asked the man, "Why (4.) _____ you so tired?"

The porter replied that he (5.) _____ extremely busy that day.

"I (6.) _____ very tired now, too," said Hunter. "It (7.) _____ Monday tomorrow. I (8.) _____ getting up very early in the morning. I hope that you (9.) _____ awake early!"

Hunter shrugged and went to look for his room. Number 407 was on the fourth floor. The agent put down his suitcase and went to open the window. The room looked out onto a house wall. The air outside had become cooler. Suddenly, a wire rope pressed coldly around Hunter's neck. The agent choked. He pushed his hand between the wire and his neck and he gasped for breath. With his other hand, he managed to grasp hold of the fingers which held the wire. He squeezed until the attacker loosened his grip. Hunter took advantage of the moment. He pulled the rope away from his neck. His attacker let go of the wire. Quickly, the agent turned around. He kicked his attacker. With a sharp karate kick, he hit the man under his chin. The man swayed, but regained his balance. Hunter was not as tall as his opponent, but was much more agile than the beefy man. His opponent took a swing at him. Nimbly, Hunter blocked his attack with a raised arm. At the same time, he kicked the man in the stomach. The blow hit home. The attacker sank to his knees. Hunter knocked him out with a karate chop to his throat.

Übung 11: Bilden Sie Genitivkonstruktionen!
Beispiel: The car belonging to the man. The man's car.

1. The decision made by the government.

2. The guns belonging to the soldiers.

3. The luggage belonging to the travellers.

4. The aeroplane belonging to the President.

5. The suggestion made by the agent.

6. The instructions given by the Captain.

"What a start!" thought the agent. He tied up the man and laid him on the bed. Then he frisked him and searched his pockets. Apart from another wire rope and a wallet, Hunter found nothing. He took both items. While the other man was still unconscious, he could not do anything. Hunter decided to go out and have dinner. He would question his prisoner later. "Somebody has definitely been expecting me," he brooded. He wondered who these people were who were giving him such a warm welcome.

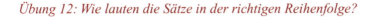

Übung 12: Wie lauten die Sätze in der richtigen Reihenfolge?

1. clock   struck   The   just   twelve   had.

___

2. It   past   a   was   five   quarter   nearly.

___

3. men   know   the   did   not   time   The.

___

4. very   the   evening   It   in   was   late.

___

5. seven   alarm   rang   clock   precisely   His   at   o'clock.

___

6. ticking   The   clock   old   was   loudly.

___

Hunter finished his meal quickly. He was tired. That morning, he had packed his suitcase, and then he had been briefed at the Secret Service Headquarters in London. After that, he had travelled to Heathrow Airport and had then spent eight hours in a cramped aeroplane. There was still something else he had to do. The man on his bed would have regained consciousness. Hunter was keen to find out who the man was and, most importantly, who had sent him.

Room 407 was empty. The sheets lay crumpled on the mattress. The prisoner had disappeared and so had the ropes that Hunter had used to tie him up. As a precaution, Hunter removed his pistol from his belt. He crept along the wall to the window and looked down. There was no evidence that the man had escaped through the window. He checked the wardrobe: empty. He also checked the small bathroom which was separated from the room by a door. He found nobody.

Übung 13: Setzen Sie diese Sätze ins Simple Past!

The agent (1. be) _____ asleep. Suddenly, he (2. wake up) _____. He (3. hear) _____ a noise in the bathroom and (4. know) _____ that the spy was in his room. Quickly, he (5. get) _____ out of bed. He (6. throw) _____ open the bathroom door. The spy (7. leap) _____ out of the shower. He (8. run) _____ to the window and (9. jump) _____ out. Then the agent (10. see) _____ a suspicious package. He (11. think) _____ it was a time bomb. Carefully, he (12. creep) _____ towards to the door. The room was very dark. After a few moments, the agent (13. find) _____ the key. He unlocked the door and (14. run) _____ quickly out of the room.

Hunter sat down on the bed and played with the weapon in his hand.
"What's going on?" he wondered. He was at a complete loss. His attacker had left no clues. What should he do? Move to a different hotel? There was no point. His attacker would have no difficulty

finding him again. So what should he do? Report back to the Secret Service Headquarters? Secure the room and let colleagues search it for clues? Hunter rejected these ideas too. Reporting back to the Secret Service would only cause trouble with his boss, Mrs Callaghan. She would accuse him of having left the attacker unguarded in a hotel room. "She would be right," Hunter thought reluctantly. Perhaps she would even threaten to transfer him to an office job again? His earlier 'promotion' to the 'Department of Internal Affairs' was still vivid in Hunter's memory. He did not want to endanger his regained freedom in external duty. Not to mention all the bureaucracy that a report would cause! No, he had to sort out the case himself. No doubt his attacker would return. "Just you wait, my friend," thought Hunter grimly. "Next time, I'll be ready!"

He bent down and reached for his suitcase. But it was not there: his luggage had disappeared along with his prisoner.

Übung 14: Setzen Sie die Sätze in die indirekte Rede!

1. "I'm not very happy," said Hunter.

Hunter   said   that

___

2. "What day is it?" asked the porter.

The   porter   asked

___

3. "I need some evidence," said the policeman.

The   policeman   said   that

___

4. "I am pleased with the results," said Mrs Callaghan.

_____

5. "I want the money!" said the thief.

_____

6. "They are extremely impolite," said the teacher.

_____

After breakfast, which he ate in one of the nearby restaurants, Hunter went to buy some new clothes.

"If things continue like this, the Secret Service expenses will be huge!" Hunter grinned at the thought. He did not mind at all. At least, not as far as his boss Mrs Callaghan was concerned. She had always been trying to trip him up. Once, he had nearly found her guilty of illegal arms dealing. Since then, she had attempted to block him whenever she had the opportunity. Hunter, in turn, was just waiting for the right moment to put an end to her corrupt wheeling and dealing.

Today, however, there were other things on the agenda. He had a meeting with Walter Brenner, an American agent. Smiling, Hunter put the Bermuda shorts back on the stand.

"Clothes like that are only for Yanks," he decided. He chose beige trekking shorts and a green T-shirt. At the till, he added a pair of sunglasses. With a satisfied glance at the three bags full of clothes, he decided to end his shopping trip. At least for now.

It was 11 o'clock in the morning and the bright sun was burning above the dusty streets of the small town. "There isn't much going on here considering it's the capital of a group of four islands," thought the agent. He walked from the hotel, which was situated at the edge of the town, to the market square in the town centre.

Übung 15: Unterstreichen Sie die Adjektive!

The alleyways were narrow and winding. Apart from a few rusty bicycles and a rickety old car or one of the black taxis here and there, there was nobody around. The whole town seemed to be asleep.

But Hunter was wrong. As he approached the town centre, he heard some noise. Reassured that there were people around after all, he continued. He had been worried that he was in the wrong place.
The demonstration in front of the church was already in full swing. Some 200 men, women and children were taking part. Some were carrying banners saying, "Mogudi is killing his children" or "We did not choose death. Down with Mogudi's Government."

Übung 16: Enträtseln Sie das Lösungswort!

1. Menschenmasse   □ _ _ _ _
2. Kriegsschiff   _ _ _ _ □ _ _
3. Gefangener   _ _ □ _ _ _ _
4. Spur/Hinweis   _ □ _ _
5. alt   _ _ □
6. Zeitung   _ _ _ _ _ _ _ □
7. Frühstück   _ _ □ _ _ _ _ _
8. Vormittag   _ _ _ □ _ _ _

Lösung: _ _ _ _ _ _ _ _

Somebody pressed a leaflet into Hunter's hand. The woman who gave it to him was a native. She asked him where he came from. Hunter used his false identity and said that his home country was Holland. She explained to him in broken English what the demonstration was about. "Mogudi's Government is carrying out weapons testing. Even if it's all being kept quiet, we know what's going on." In a sweeping gesture, the woman indicated the group of people who were now chanting, "Down with the weapons. Down with the weapons."

The woman, who was wearing a summer skirt and a light blouse, continued, "This week two fishermen died during a weapons test. Officially it was an accident at sea. I ask you, we have been fishermen for generations!"

She thrust another leaflet into his hand and disappeared into the crowd.

The leaflet confirmed what Hunter already knew. His immediate boss in London, Captain Martens, had explained to him what was going on: illegal weapons testing on the islands. However, other international secret services suspected that it was not only the island's Government which was behind it all.

Übung 17: Unterstreichen Sie die Adverbien im Text!

Suddenly, Hunter felt a hand on his shoulder and an object pressed into his back. He turned around quickly and wanted to throw a punch. Walter Brenner laughed loudly. "Hi!" he shouted and grabbed Hunter's right hand. He shook it violently. He seemed to be waiting for the Englishman to say something.

Hunter eyed Brenner. Irritated, he noted that the American was not wearing Bermudas but short trekking trousers like he was.

"So much for prejudices," thought Hunter privately. "So this is the demonstration?" he said out loud.

Brenner nodded gravely. "Yes, there have been demonstrations like this every Tuesday and Thursday for the last two weeks."

A surge went through the demonstrators and the two agents were pushed from left to right.

"Should we go somewhere else?" suggested Hunter. Before Brenner could reply, the crowd started moving. People were shouting. The banners and placards fell, many of them onto the heads of the people below them. Children were crying loudly. The women were shrieking. Men's voices roared out. Hunter and Brenner were pushed into the middle of the square.

A distorted voice screeched out of a megaphone. "This demonstration is not permitted. Go home!"

The chaos became worse. There were crackling noises from the megaphone and then the men heard, "This is the police speaking. If you do not stop the demonstration immediately, we will intervene. The army has already surrounded the square."

Übung 18: Bilden Sie Sätze mit dem Komparativ!
Beispiel: man/woman (tall) The man is taller than the woman.

1. orange/pineapple (cheap)

_____

2. captain/cook (rich)

_____

3. rabbit/tortoise (fast)

_____

4. bungalow/skyscraper (low)

_____

5. chair/sofa (hard)

_____

Suddenly, there were stones flying. Hunter pushed his way out. He had lost sight of his American colleague in the crowds. All he wanted was to get out. The panic increased. A woman near him was screaming at the top of her voice. She was pulling at something lying on the ground. She was unable to lift it as there were so many bodies pressed around her.

Hunter's muscular arms pushed the people away. The woman kept shouting and pulling. The agent helped her. Now he realised that she had been holding a three-year-old boy in her hand the whole time. There was red blood beneath the child's dark hair. Hunter took the boy into his arms. The woman started to hit the agent hysterically. He grabbed her hand and pulled her along behind him. As they moved forward, he protected the boy as well as he could. The child's small body hung limply in his arms.

Hunter pushed ahead. He had almost reached the church when a new surge went through the demonstrators. From behind there were more and more shouts. He heard voices saying something about water cannons. More stones rained down on them.

The woman whimpered. She stopped suddenly when the agent spoke to her in her own language. Then she started crying again. Hunter did not know whether she had understood him or not. He had started learning the language in a crash course only two weeks earlier. It was also terribly noisy.

They reached the stone wall of the church which formed one side of the market square. Hunter wanted to move along the wall until he came to the edge of the demonstrators. He could hardly breathe. More and more people were pushing behind him. Hunter let go of the woman. With his free hand, he pushed himself powerfully along the wall. The child was between him and the stone wall. He would not give up. His arm began to tremble with the effort. The woman at his side continued howling.

*Übung 19: Setzen Sie **after** oder **before** richtig ein!*

(1.) _____ he went to the island, Hunter wanted to learn Spanish. He went to the library to borrow a book. He had been to the library many times (2.) _____. (3.) _____ a few moments, he found the right bookshelf. He located a good textbook and took it to the desk. "You must bring the book back (4.) _____ the 20th of August," said the librarian. "If you bring it back (5.) _____ that date, there will be a fine to pay." Hunter nodded. He decided to return the book (6.) _____ the end of the week (7.) _____ he had finished reading it.

All at once, the pushing from behind stopped. The rows of demonstrators immediately in front of the church thinned out. Hunter's arm was tired. He continued to hold the child in his other arm. He looked at the boy. The child's eyes were looking at the agent's face. His breathing was hot and irregular.

Suddenly, the woman ripped the child away from him. She cradled the boy in her arms and spoke to him. Hunter turned around. The market square was empty. The demonstrators had moved away to both sides. There were several bodies on the cobbles. When Hunter looked up again, he saw a lorry with a cannon on the roof at the far side of the square. The word 'water cannon' flashed through his mind. He pushed the woman with the child to one side. Taken by surprise, she tried to defend herself, but Hunter's arm pushed her forwards to a safer position. He stopped for a moment to catch his breath.

His ribs made a cracking noise as the jet of water hit him. He was slammed against the wall. His head hit the stones. His knees gave in and he fell to the ground.

Übung 20: Übersetzen Sie!

1. Die Leute standen vor der Kirche.

2. Er hielt das Kind in seinem Arm.

3. Der Agent betrachtete das Kind.

4. Der Polizist war sehr böse.

5. Die Offiziere trugen schwarze Stiefel.

When Hunter woke up, he was in pain. He could hardly turn his head. However, he could see that he was in his hotel room. He wanted to get out of bed. The air in the room was unbearably hot. He groaned loudly. Even the slightest movement was torture.

"Don't be so sorry for yourself, colleague," shouted Brenner from the bathroom. He came into the room with a cold compress and laid it on Hunter's forehead. Hunter groaned again.

"And I always thought that you Brits were brave," taunted the American.

"We are," croaked Hunter between his teeth.

Brenner was shorter and stockier than Hunter. His fair hair was poking out from under his baseball cap. 'Cleveland Indians' was written in red on the blue material. The face of a Red Indian grinned above the words. Walter Brenner had been a fan of his home city team virtually since he had been born.

"What are we going to do?" he asked Hunter.

Hunter groaned again.

Übung 21: Wie lauten die Adjektive zu den Substantiven?

1. pain _____

2. intelligence _____

3. happiness _____

4. consideration _____

5. cheerfulness _____

6. importance _____

It was already late afternoon when Hunter finally felt able to get up. His head was still throbbing but the pain in his ribs was now only a dull ache. He had no broken bones. At least, that was what he hoped. He left the hotel with his American colleague. They were both hungry.

In the hotel room, Walter had explained in detail what the American Secret Service knew about the situation. It was almost as much as the British Secret Service. In other words, hardly anything.

Because the group of islands was near American territorial waters in the Pacific, the US authorities closely monitored the islands. They kept track of trade, traffic and political activities. When Mogudi's Government had taken over the military regime on the islands several years earlier, the secret monitoring by the Americans had become more relaxed. They had high expectations for the democratically-elected Government.

The islanders, too, were enthusiastic about their new Government. That was obvious from their participation in the demonstrations, which had been held regularly for some time. As far as Walter knew, the earlier demonstrations had ended with the same riots as had occurred that day. Deaths and injuries were always the result once the army and the police intervened to stop the demonstration by employing violence.

! *Übung 22: Welcher Satz enthält die richtige Zeitform? Kreuzen Sie die Lösung an!*

ÜBUNG 22

1. Sein Kopf dröhnte.
   a) ☐ His head will throb.
   b) ☐ His head is throbbing.
   c) ☐ His head was throbbing.

2. Walter hatte die Situation bereits dargelegt.
   a) ☐ Walter had already described the situation.
   b) ☐ Walter was already describing the situation.
   c) ☐ Walter is already describing the situation.

3. Sie wissen genau, was passiert.
   a) ☐ They knew exactly what was happening.
   b) ☐ They knew exactly what would happen.
   c) ☐ They know exactly what is happening.

4. Die Regierung war sehr streng geworden.
   a) ☐ The Government was becoming very strict.
   b) ☐ The Government had become very strict.
   c) ☐ The Government is becoming very strict.

5. Wir werden nie zufrieden sein.
   a) ☐ We have never been satisfied.
   b) ☐ We are never satisfied.
   c) ☐ We will never be satisfied.

The two agents entered the pub. The narrow room was dimly lit and extended back from the door. They heard muted jazz music. Hunter was surprised. Once again, he had expected Bob Marley or similar. Walter seemed to guess what he was thinking. "Not reggae, then?" he grinned. "This pub is a bit of local knowledge. I've been stationed undercover here for three years now. How do you think I've managed? Only beaches and palm trees and pina colada? No thanks!" He sat down at one of the corner tables made of dark wood. Hunter sat opposite him. The wooden chairs were uncomfortable but he liked the atmosphere in the pub.

There were not many other diners. It was only five o'clock. Walter explained that the islanders did not usually eat before nine or ten o'clock in the evening.

"Is there anything to eat then?" enquired Hunter. He had not eaten anything since his breakfast. After everything that had happened at the demonstration, he felt ravenous and had a headache.

Übung 23: Formulieren Sie die Sätze im Passiv!
Beispiel: The thief stole the money.
    The money was stolen by the thief.

1. The agent opened the suitcase lid.

2. The man read the newspaper.

3. The Captain shouted the orders.

4. The demonstrators waved the banners.

5. The tourist ordered a taxi.

6. The agent wrote the report.

A waiter in a casual shirt, shorts and sandals came to their table and placed two dog-eared menus in front of them. He waited as if he expected them to know what they wanted without even looking at the menus. The Englishman grabbed one and began to look through it. "What's 'scampi sorpresa'?" he wanted to know.

"None left," answered the waiter abruptly. When he saw that the agent wanted to ask another question, he interrupted, "None of that left either." Then he was silent.

"No wonder there are no tourists here," thought Hunter. "How can people be so unfriendly?"

Übung 24: Setzen Sie das richtige Pronomen ein!
(mine, yours, his, hers, ours, theirs)

1. I own that shirt. That shirt is _____.

2. The waiter was wearing shorts. The shorts were _____.

3. The officers had guns. The guns were _____.

4. You own that restaurant. That restaurant is _____.

5. "The house belongs to that woman," he said. "It's _____.

6. We have now bought our tickets. The tickets are _____.

7. The agent had a suitcase. The suitcase was _____.

8. The demonstrators were shouting. "This island is _____," they chanted.

9. "That food belongs to me," said Hunter. "It's _____!"

Walter was unperturbed by the waiter's unhelpfulness. He winked at him. "What do you recommend? We're hungry!"
"We've got fish today," said the waiter.

31

"Great!" said Walter. "And two white wine spritzers as well."
Hunter looked curiously at Walter. Walter shrugged. "That's normal here. When in Rome, do as the Romans do, I always say."
The other man was not sure whether he really did want to get used to it. However, when he tasted the delicately-grilled fish fillet, he was happy. The rice, which was generously heaped on the plate, was wonderfully tender. So were the vegetables. They were in a sauce which was exactly the right combination of sweet and sour.
"Delicious!" exclaimed Hunter with his mouth full.
After the meal, they ordered two espressos.

Übung 25: Welche Phrasen gehören zusammen?

1. When in Rome, do as the Romans do.
2. He lives in a world of his own.
3. It's all Greek to me.
4. The world's your oyster.
5. Rome was not built in a day.
6. He felt on top of the world.
7. He's in the land of Nod.
8. It's not the end of the world!

a) ☐ Great achievements require great effort.
b) ☐ You have lots of opportunities.
c) ☐ Worse things could happen.
d) ☐ He was extremely happy.
e) ☐ To act the same way as the local people.
f) ☐ He's asleep.
g) ☐ He likes day-dreaming.
h) ☐ I don't understand.

As they drank their coffee, Hunter summarised what they knew.
"We strongly suspect that there is illegal weapons testing being carried out here. There have been demonstrations by environmentalists which have been broken up with violence. That means that the environmentalists have the same suspicions as we do. There are the two dead fishermen and an Argentinian warship in the harbour."
Hunter's colleague continued, "There are some reports from American surveillance stations that Cesare Mogudi has business relations primarily with Argentina, Russia and Great Britain. The Government also seems to have political allies in the USA, China and some smaller countries in East Europe. At least, there are diplomats from these countries on the island."
"What does your Diplomat think about Mogudi?" probed Hunter.
"I'm careful with Mitchell," said the Secret Service man. "At first I thought he was onto a good job here, on this tropical island with all the palm trees. But something is not quite right. In the Secret Service, we're on our guard. Some of our men and women are not here officially in their role as agents. They are undercover as administrative employees."

Übung 26: Verwenden Sie die Kurzform!

1. The environmentalists are unhappy. (They are) _____ displeased with the Government.

2. (There is) _____ an Argentinian warship in the harbour.

3. (He is) _____ very suspicious of his colleague.

4. His boss is called Mrs Callaghan. (She is) _____ very strict.

5. (We are) _____ going to inform the Government.

Hunter smiled. In the block of flats where he lived in London, his neighbours thought that he worked in the Finance Department of the city authorities. The Secret Service had given him this false identity when he started his job. He had got used to it in the meantime and now it was often difficult for him to assume a different identity.

He had arrived on the island undercover as a Dutch businessman. His Dutch was quite acceptable, but he somehow liked the middle-class aura which the role of a finance administrator gave him.

Walter continued. "So, we're shadowing our own people from the Diplomatic Corps. Perhaps it's different for you in England. Surely you prefer honour and the nation and the Queen?"

Hunter replied, "What are you talking about? It's just as corrupt in our country as it is anywhere else. And don't go asking me what schemes the sycophants in Buckingham Palace are cooking up now!"

Walter raised his coffee cup. "Then I suggest that we begin our international teamwork!"

Hunter raised his cup. "To us!"

Übung 27: Fügen Sie im folgenden Absatz alle Satzzeichen ein!

So where do you work asked his neighbour

I work for the city authorities replied Hunter This was not the truth but as a Secret Service man he had to be careful You never knew who was a spy

Gosh replied the man That is a coincidence I work for them too What Department are you in

Hunter told his neighbour that he worked in the Finance Department. Then he turned and went into his flat He could not face any more awkward questions

The door of the pub opened with a dull thud. "Down!" yelled a woman wearing a scarf over her face. Only her eyes could be seen through the two thin slits. Her stocky frame was dressed in dark overalls. Three men stood behind her. They all held drawn pistols in their hands.

Quick as lightning, Hunter and Walter slid from their chairs and hid underneath the table. They both had their weapons ready.

"If this is supposed to be a raid," said the waiter, "then you're too late. There were a couple of crooks here yesterday."

"Shut up!" The woman's voice was surprisingly deep. It did not seem to match her small face.

"OK, then!" said the waiter. He seemed to be used to events like this.

"Where are your foreign visitors?" she asked. Her companions began to swarm around the room. The agents under the table looked nervously at each other.

"They're at the back at the corner table." The waiter obligingly gave her the information. When he saw that the men were no longer there, he added, "Or were …."

Übung 28: Unterstreichen Sie das „schwarze Schaf"!

1. chair, seat, bench, stool, table
2. overalls, scarf, suitcase, uniform, cap, jacket
3. face, wound, neck, forehead, elbow, thigh
4. stocky, strong, burly, muscular, fat, weak
5. pistol, rifle, ship, machine gun, missile, torpedo

The two agents jumped up at the same time. They pushed the table towards the armed men who were approaching them. Then they took advantage of the confusion and dashed between the shocked attackers to the door. The woman was the first to regain her composure.

"Shoot!" she shouted. At the same time, she fired a shot which barely missed Hunter's head. A second shot followed, but it missed him too.

Walter was already at the door and gave cover to Hunter who was behind him. He fired several shots into the room. One of the men groaned. Hunter thought he recognised the voice. He looked more closely at the wounded man. He wore a dark suit and the scarf he wore over his face was similar to the leader's scarf. From his build, the agent thought he recognised the man whom he had caught in his hotel room.

Hunter had no more time to think about the matter. Walter was holding the door open and shouting at him to hurry up. Before he managed to run out of the pub, a bullet flew past his ear and embedded itself in the wall. Walter shouted again, not to tell Hunter to hurry up, but in pain. A shot had injured his arm.

Übung 29: Setzen Sie die Komparativform ein!

1. The woman's voice was loud but the man's voice was _____.

2. The agent's aim was good but the soldier's aim was _____.

3. The service in the café was bad but the service in the restaurant was _____.

4. There were many soldiers on the warship but there were _____ soldiers on the aircraft carrier.

5. The waiter was old but the barman was even _____.

6. The coffee cost little but the tea cost _____.

The Englishman slipped behind Walter through the door. It slammed shut noisily as they both ran outside.

The agents hurried down the street. Night was falling. Here, in the side street, the tarmac had large potholes and they had to be careful that they did not fall.

Their pursuers clattered after them. There were three taxis at the side of the road. The drivers stood together in front of one, chatting and smoking. Quickly, Hunter and Walter jumped into the taxi at the end of the queue. Expertly Hunter grasped the cable below the steering wheel and short-circuited the car. The motor sprang to life and he pulled out of the parking space.

They heard violent swearing. The taxi drivers had noticed the theft and also wanted to pursue the agents. There was the sound of three shots; the taxi drivers had been stopped dead in their tracks. The masked woman and her companions climbed into the other two taxis and raced after the agents' car.

Hunter had no idea where he was going.

"Where to?" he shouted. When Walter said nothing, he repeated, "Where to?"

"Damn! It's sore!" groaned his colleague, holding his arm.

"And I thought you Americans were brave?" joked Hunter.

"Very funny!" was all Walter could say.

Hunter drove on. The car bumped over the potholes. The bodywork rattled and creaked. His foot pressed the accelerator down to the floor. The car could not go any faster. In the rear mirror, he saw the two other cars approaching. The agents' lead was narrowing.

Übung 30: Finden Sie Synonyme zu den Wörtern in Klammern!

"Where are we actually going?" (1. asked) _____ Walter. Surprised, Hunter (2. answered) _____, "I thought you knew your way around here?" In the meantime, they had (3. arrived at) _____ the edge of the town. There was a fork in the road. A narrow track (4. led) _____ down to the beach. A wider road led up towards the cliffs. Hunter (5. chose) _____ this road. Their pursuers were close behind them.

The (6. noise) _____ of bullets came from behind. Two or three shots (7. struck) _____ the metal of the car.

"Enough is enough!" Walter decided. He wound down the window and held out his gun. He shot behind him over his shoulder. There was a dull thud: he had hit his target. One of tyres on the pursuers' car had burst.

The agents heard persistent honking. In the rear mirror, Hunter saw that the car immediately behind them was skidding. It was spinning around at the side of the road. Then it came to a standstill at the very edge of the precipice. The second taxi braked hard. It collided with bits of the burst tyre which were lying in the road. It then left the road and collided against the first taxi. The first taxi rocked backwards and forwards for a moment and then fell over the cliff into the sea.

Hunter drove on, racing along the coast. As soon as he was sure that nobody was still chasing them, he stopped.

"Somebody knows that we're here," he said.

His colleague corrected him. "Somebody knows *you're* here. I've been here for years and there haven't been any incidents like this until now."

Hunter retorted, "Well, you obviously hadn't uncovered any great mysteries until now, had you?"

"Excuse me," said the other man. Then he changed his mind. Hunter was right. His life as an agent here on the island had been rather peaceful. However, it was clear that the peace and quiet had now come to an end.

Übung 31: Setzen Sie die richtige Präposition ein!
(above, over, below, under)

1. The bullet flew _____ the roof of the car.

2. Hunter was hiding _____ his coat.

3. He was wearing a shirt _____ his jacket.

4. The driver drove _____ the potholes.

5. The plane flew high _____ the clouds.

6. There was a large town _____ .

Hunter wanted to take Walter to the hospital, but the American refused. "You're not going to sew it up yourself, are you?" asked the Englishman.

"Well, we Americans, we're tough blokes," Walter said seriously. He looked at Hunter's shocked expression. "Rubbish!" he said. "A woman I know is a doctor in a hospital. It belongs to a Foreign Aid Centre. It's got a school and homes for orphans. Humanitarian aid.

To get the political support of the recipient country. You know what I mean." Hunter nodded. Walter gave him directions to the Foreign Aid Centre and they made their way their.

When they had arrived, Hunter almost regretted that his headache had completely disappeared. He liked the look of the female doctor who welcomed Walter. Her blonde hair was tied in a bun at the back of her head. Two strands had come loose and framed her face. Her warm brown eyes made Hunter's heart beat faster. He decided secretly that he would get a few gunshot wounds the next time too.

ÜBUNG 32 !

*Übung 32: Verbinden Sie die Sätze mit **who**!*
Beispiel: The Americans are arriving. They are carrying flags.
The Americans who are arriving are carrying flags.

1. The agent drives the car. He is serious.

_____

2. The woman works in the hospital. She is a doctor.

_____

3. The nurses come from Europe. They are well-trained.

_____

4. The doctors work long hours. They are very tired.

_____

5. The receptionist is writing. She has brown hair.

_____

Hunter left his colleague in the doctor's care and promised to return the next day to collect him. Now he had to get back to the hotel. He had still not sent a report to the Headquarters in London. He would do that next. He also had to make other preparations. Early the next morning, he wanted to take a closer look at the Argentinian warship. After that, he had to collect Walter and plan with him what they should do. Perhaps it would be worth breaking into the ship during the night? He would decide tomorrow when he saw the ship. Back in his room, he took some security precautions. The porter had handed him his key without a word as he had done the previous evening. He was no help when it came to security. He let anybody into the hotel. That was, if he could be bothered to rouse himself from the adjoining room to come to the desk.

Hunter entered room number 407 with his gun drawn. This time, nobody had secretly entered his room. There was no one waiting for him. Nevertheless, he had to protect his room with a few security measures. His suitcase had disappeared along with his clothing, and so had his mobile alarm system, portable computer, satellite system and other weapons and pieces of equipment. The only things he had were the contents of his coat pockets and his blue rucksack.

Taking a reel of wire from his coat pocket, Hunter unwound a length and then stretched it from the bed across the room as a trip wire. Because the room door opened inwards, he could not attach the wire directly behind the door. He then took a book from the rucksack which had been his hand luggage on the aeroplane. He leaned the book upright against the closed door. If somebody opened the door, the book would fall. He would hear it and his gun, which he would place beside his pillow, would be ready.

With the same intention, he placed the second volume of his reading material on the sash window which opened onto the house wall opposite.

ÜBUNG 33

Übung 33: Welche Verben und Substantive gehören zusammen?

1. to load
2. to give
3. to ask
4. to write
5. to knit
6. to take
7. to eat
8. to welcome

a) ☐ an aspirin
b) ☐ a gun
c) ☐ a meal
d) ☐ a visitor
e) ☐ a letter
f) ☐ a jumper
g) ☐ a presentation
h) ☐ a question

In London, his assistant, Percy Horn, lifted the receiver. Hunter briefly described the situation and asked the junior agent to pass on his report to Captain Martens and to the Director of the Secret Service, Mrs Callaghan. The older man had been expecting Percy to listen enviously to his adventures. Percy, however, only seemed to be listening with half an ear.

"Well," he said cheerfully, "tomorrow, I'm off! Two weeks of sun, sea and sand, fantastic …"

It was a few seconds before Hunter understood what Percy was saying. "Are you going on holiday, Horn?"

"Yes, I'm travelling to the Caribbean. To a club with all the trimmings. Since you're not here at the moment, there's not much I can do."

"You can help me from London. The matter is much trickier than we expected."

Percy was uncertain as he said, "Is it?"

Hunter continued speaking into his mobile. "The bullets are flying around my head here and you're taking a holiday!"

Percy sounded confused. "I'm sorry, if you don't want me to go … If you want me to stay … I can go on holiday in London. Then it would be easier to reach me. Or I needn't bother with a holiday. Yes, I'll not bother. Then I'll be here all the time for you. That is, if you need something."

"Horn!" interjected the other man. "You go to your club and enjoy yourself. I was only joking! I'm fine, honestly. And a few bullets have never harmed an agent. Go and enjoy yourself! And if you take part in a show, bring me a video of it, won't you?"

*Übung 34: Setzen Sie **to, two** oder **too** ein!*

"Tomorrow, I'm off!" he said. (1.) "_____ weeks of sun, sea and sand! I'm going (2.) _____ the Caribbean. I'm travelling (3.) _____ the airport by taxi with my (4.) _____ suitcases and my camera (5.) _____. I hope the taxi won't be (6.) _____ expensive (7.) _____ get there. It costs a lot of money (8.) _____ travel by taxi these days! But it would be (9.) _____ bad if I missed the aeroplane (10.) _____ my destination. Would you like to come (11.) _____ ?"

As he walked towards the docks the next morning, Hunter thought that the blue overalls suited him quite well. He had bought them as soon as the shop had opened. He could only find one clothes shop in the small town. The choice was extremely limited. He had chosen these blue dungarees and a dark knitted hat. Despite the heat here, the people seemed to be fond of wearing hats.

His observation was confirmed by the workers he passed at the docks. They all wore headwear, mostly in Rasta colours. Hunter wondered briefly whether he should go back to the hotel. All the men were black. He was worried that, as a white person and, into the bargain, a pale Englishman, he stood out.

However, nobody seemed particularly interested in him and his appearance. He strolled along the docks. Walter had told him roughly where he would find the Argentinian warship. It was berthed at a quay towards the back of the harbour. The huge iron hull rose out of the water in front of the agent. A rickety wooden ladder led from the quay onto the deck. He could see a couple of men on the deck but they were not paying him any attention. Hunter could not see anybody who seemed interested in what was happening on the quay.

Übung 35: Setzen Sie diese Verben ins Simple Past!

1. tell _____
2. say _____
3. hear _____
4. cry _____
5. leave _____
6. think _____
7. hit _____
8. dig _____
9. sing _____
10. freeze _____

A man wearing a hat came towards him. "She's big, isn't she?"
Hunter replied, "Yes, huge. What sort of ship is she?"
The dockworker seemed pleased to have found somebody whom he could impress with his knowledge. "She's definitely at least twenty years old. But she's in excellent shape. They made things

differently back then. The Germans are very good when it comes to warships."

Hunter asked, "The Germans? Isn't that an Argentinian flag?"

"Yes," said the other man patronisingly, "she sails under the Argentinian flag now, but she was built in Germany. The Argentinian navy bought her eleven years ago." He paused for effect. Then he provided some facts and figures on how the ship was constructed and equipped. He seemed to know all about it.

"How do you know all this?" enquired Hunter.

"Tomorrow they're hiring new people for a special mission or something. People for below decks, the engine room and so on. It seems as though the soldiers up there don't want to do any of the dirty work." The man pointed towards the deck of the ship. Before Hunter could say anything, the dockworker continued, "And so I said to myself, apply! That's why I found out about the ship in case they question me. I'm applying tomorrow." He looked proudly at Hunter. "Hey man, keep your fingers crossed! They pay well, you know!"

Thinking quickly, Hunter asked, "What time tomorrow and where do you have to report?"

The man beamed. He seemed to like the prospect of having Hunter as a colleague below decks. Willingly he told him what he knew about how and where to apply.

Then he said goodbye cheerfully. He still had work to do at Dock 17. "But I won't need that job much longer," he shouted over his shoulder as he walked away.

Hunter looked at him briefly. Satisfied with the information he had acquired, he put his hands in his pockets and turned to the warship again. His plan was clear.

"From tomorrow, I'm a sailor," he decided.

ÜBUNG 36

Übung 36: Setzen Sie diese Verben ins Present Continuous!

The dockworker (1. wear) _____ black boots.

The tools he (2. carry) _____ look very heavy.

Nevertheless, the man (3. whistle) _____ cheerfully.

He (4. look) _____ for his colleagues. They (5. work)

_____ at a different dock. They (6. repair) _____

an old cargo ship. The ship (7. near) _____ the end

of its life and the workers (8. try) _____ to salvage it.

A soldier dressed in camouflage appeared at the deck rail. He cupped his hands in front of his mouth and shouted down to the quay, "Hey, man, what's going on?"

Hunter was surprised at how fluent his Spanish still was as he answered the man, "Nothing, nothing. I'm just looking at your ship here. She's a fine vessel."

The soldier was pleased and said, "She's a fine ship inside as well."

The piercing shout of the soldier's boss rang out. The soldier disappeared immediately without saying goodbye. Hunter was left alone.

He looked around the quay for a short time and then left the harbour. It was time to return to the hotel. He had to change his clothes, get a car and fetch Walter.

ÜBUNG 37

*Übung 37: Formulieren Sie die Sätze mit **can** oder **could**!*

1. He was able to see the ship.

2. Hunter was able to speak Spanish.

_____

3. The soldiers were able to shoot very well.

_____

4. The Captain is able to shout extremely loudly.

_____

5. The ship was able to carry a large amount of ammunition.

_____

6. The torpedoes are able to detonate automatically.

_____

It took some time to organise a car. The taxi the agents had stolen the evening before had disappeared. Hunter had just left it two streets away from the hotel. However, he was no longer surprised that things went missing as simply as that. The small town really was quite peculiar.

In his room, he changed out of his dungarees into a light-coloured linen suit. The suit was another new purchase which he had added to his expenses list after the theft of his belongings. The column for 'Clothing, general' on the list was growing.

In his role as a Dutch businessman, he asked the sullen porter whether there was a car hire company nearby. The porter was not helpful at all. Hunter's question was too much for him. Apart from a grumpy "No idea," the man said nothing. Hunter sighed.

Übung 38: Lesen Sie weiter und bilden Sie sinnvolle Wörter!

Hunter made his way into the town (1. enetcr) _____. He had seen a tourist (2. onrimafntio) _____ office during his first visit to the (3. tamerk) _____ square. At least, he thought he could remember one. His (4. mcstaoh) _____ was rumbling. He stopped at a (5. kebray) _____, but it was (6. ldocse) _____. The sign said that (7. mlutniche) _____ was from eleven o'clock until four o'clock, presumably (8. baeuces) _____ of the heat.

Sweating under the material of his jacket, he continued walking. The streets were empty now too. There was nothing happening in the square in front of the church. He wondered briefly what had become of the woman with the small boy.

The market square was enclosed by white-painted arcades in the colonial style which gave the scene an imperial air. Strangely, however, the walls seemed to bear no traces of age.

"It looks more like a recent colonial-style renovation," thought the agent. He walked in the shade of the arcades. The cool air which had gathered there made him feel better. He had walked almost all the way around the square when he noticed the sign for the information office. He had been right.

The employees were not at lunch here, but the office was closed. Hesitantly, Hunter stood in front of the window. Its only decoration was white curtains. "No wonder there are no holidaymakers here," he thought again.

A woman came through the arcades towards to him. After a moment, Hunter recognised who she was. It was the woman who had given him the leaflet during the demonstration. A smile came over her serious face when she realised who he was.
"Oh, hello, it's you again," she began.
Hunter was amazed. She was not in the least bit shy. As an Englishman, this felt quite strange to him. He tried to remember his last date with a woman but could not. He gave up and turned to the woman. She was in her early forties and was small and round. There was a joyful expression on her brown face, which was framed by dark curls. Hunter thought she looked like his neighbour, Rosie Carpenter. He would send Rosie and her little daughter Ginny a postcard. Later.
"You're not from here, are you?", asked the woman. "I noticed that straightaway."
Hunter confirmed her observation and told her that he was a businessman from Europe. She liked the word 'Holland' even though she admitted that she had never heard of the country. When Hunter explained to her that he was looking for a car hire company, she took his arm. "Come with me. I'll sort it out," was all she said.
She led the agent through the streets and alleyways. A few minutes later, Hunter had lost his sense of direction. He at least wanted to know where he was going. Stray dogs lay asleep in front of the house doors. Two or three dogs were sharing a small patch of shade. In other places, the animals were stretched out in the blazing sunshine. Life here was strangely peaceful. The woman kept talking while they walked. She wanted to know everything about Holland. Hunter slowly learnt who she was. Her name was Lily and she was a teacher in a secondary school. She was interested in literature, culture and politics.
Hunter kept trying to stop his companion's flow of conversation.

He was interested in finding out about the demonstrations. However, Lily changed the topic every time he asked about it. She wanted to organise the car first.

Übung 39: Stellen Sie passende Fragen zu den Antworten! (Verwenden Sie how, where, who, what, whose, how much)

1. My neighbour is Rosie Carpenter.

   _____

2. Her daughter's name is Ginny.

   _____

3. Rosie lives in the flat opposite me.

   _____

4. I am very tired.

   _____

5. The ticket costs £100.00.

   _____

6. I'm staying in a shabby hotel on Strand Street.

   _____

7. That's my house!

   _____

8. The dogs sleep on the pavement.

   _____

Half an hour later, Hunter was sitting on Lily's sofa beneath a whirring fan. The living room in the small house was cramped. The walls were painted canary yellow. Everything was brightly coloured: the sofa, the cupboard, the carpet. There were flowers with colourful petals in a wide vase on the table.

Lily's two sons, aged 11 and 8, were sitting on the floor. Her mother and her sister, who had two small girls, twins about three years old, were also there. Lily's husband worked for a shipping company. He worked in an office. Her younger brother, a student, was also staying at the house. Lily ran quickly out of the room to fetch him. Ignoring his protests, she told him to go immediately to the harbour and collect her husband's car.

With a wave of her hand, Lily dismissed Hunter's objection about borrowing her private car. He was her guest, she told him.

Übung 40: Lesen Sie weiter und setzen Sie die richtigen Konjunktionen ein!

(both … and, although, and, either … or, while, because)

Lily served freshly-squeezed lemonade (1.) _____ banana chips. The chips could be dipped into (2.) _____ a sweet-and-sour sauce (3.) _____ a hot sauce. (4.) _____ he was ravenous, Hunter was reserved at first. Then, (5.) _____ everybody else was eating, he started helping himself enthusiastically. The snacks were (6.) _____ delicious (7.) _____ very filling. (8.) _____ they waited, Lily began to explain what was happening.

"We are demonstrating because we are fed up. Mogudi's Government is even worse than the military dictatorship which we had to put up with before. At first everything looked all right when Mogudi became Governor two years ago. But since then …."

Lily's sister started to speak. "It's unbearable now. The beaches on the other side of the island are closed off. There's supposed to be a conservation area there."

"It's ridiculous!" interjected the grandmother, who was sitting next to Hunter on the sofa. She could not stop looking at the foreigner. She liked having somebody so exotic in her house. Without any scruples, she stared directly at him. When he returned her gaze, she beamed, delighted.

Übung 41: Enträtseln Sie das Lösungswort!

1. gegen
2. Bevölkerung
3. Wähler
4. Rede
5. für
6. Politiker
7. Mitglied
8. wählen
9. Kandidat
10. Wahlkreis

Lösung: _ _ _ _ _ _ _ _ _ _

Lily took up the story. "The beaches are closed off because they're contaminated. Everyone here knows that. At the beginning, it was only aircraft carriers or submarines carrying out their manoeuvres here. Our country doesn't have its own navy; we co-operate with other nations. At least, that's what I think. Recently, there have been more and more warships."

While Lily's sister wiped one of the little girls' mouths, she said, "Our country actually consists of four main islands. Until a few months ago, they were all occupied. Now two of the islands have been evacuated. The people from them are living here now."

"It's ridiculous!" said the grandmother again, angrily.

"No, it's dreadful!" corrected her daughter, Lily. "Some of the resettled women were about to give birth when they were brought here. Someone my husband knows is a doctor. What he says about the births is horrific. Totally deformed children. I'll spare you the details."

Hunter put the banana chip he was holding back on the plate. He was horrified at what he was hearing. He had lost his appetite completely. Lily continued, "The Government took these children away as soon as they were born. Supposedly to a care home. However, my husband's friend is quite certain that those children were killed. He made some enquiries. It seems as though it's all due to nuclear radiation."

"We don't want any nuclear testing here! We don't want a Government which abuses our country like this!" cried the grandmother. "Do we have an army anyway?" she asked suddenly.

"That's exactly the point, mama," said Lily. "We don't have one. So what does it all mean? Why would we need nuclear bombs? Who's going to attack us? Do the people in Holland think that we're a threat?" Lily looked at Hunter.

Hunter had to laugh at the question. He disregarded the taxi drivers at the airport, the porter at the hotel and the waiter. He forgot about the visitor to his room when he arrived and the armed gang in the pub and said, "No, you're not a threat here at all." To prove his words, he took the banana chip which he had placed back on the plate. He dipped it forcefully into the sauce.

He started to cough loudly. He had dipped the chip into the hot sauce. "Delicious!" he coughed. There were tears in his eyes and his mouth was burning.

Übung 42: Schreiben Sie die Sätze ganz aus!

1. Our country doesn't have its own army.

_____

2. That isn't what I think.

_____

3. He wasn't surprised.

_____

4. I won't give you the details.

_____

5. We don't want any nuclear testing!

_____

6. They wouldn't listen to us.

_____

Lily's brother arrived with the car. The family did not listen to Hunter when he said that he would hire a car. And they did not want to accept any money for the loan of their car. In fact, Hunter had the feeling that he had offended the family with his offer to pay. Quickly, he praised the car.

Lily pressed the keys into his hand. She assured him again that he could borrow it until the following weekend.

"Are you coming to the demonstration in the market square tomorrow?" she enquired as he got in.

"If I can, yes," answered Hunter.

Übung 43: Bilden Sie Wortfamilien!

das Adjektiv: slow

1. der Komparativ: _____   3. das Adverb: _____

2. der Superlativ: _____   4. das Substantiv: _____

das Adjektiv: beautiful

1. der Komparativ: _____   3. das Adverb: _____

2. der Superlativ: _____   4. das Substantiv: _____

The old car spluttered when he started the engine. It seemed to be held together by rust. However, it moved and that was the most important thing. Hunter turned the jalopy onto the coast road. As he drove past the spot where his pursuers' car had fallen over the precipice the day before, he shuddered. They were fighting with no holds barred.

The Foreign Aid Centre was peaceful as Hunter parked in the yard.

Gravel crunched under his feet as he walked from the car to the entrance door of the hospital. The building was no larger than an ordinary house. It was like Lily's house. Only here, the roof was covered with straw instead of wooden tiles.

Übung 44: Unterstreichen Sie die Synonyme der Wörter in Klammern!
(1. made a swishing noise 2. brown-haired 3. perfect 4. a tropical grass 5. a single flower 6. grabbed 7. medical dressing)

A ceiling fan whirred quietly. The floor had just been mopped. On the walls there were photos of smiling children with dark curls and wide eyes and, between them, blonde and brunette nurses in white coats. Hunter thought it was almost too idyllic.

There was a vase of flowers on the bamboo desk in the reception area. Hunter stole a stem with particularly bright petals. He wanted to give it to the young doctor.

However, when Walter came out to greet he colleague, he snatched the flower from Hunter with his uninjured hand. His other arm was covered by a white bandage. "Thank you. You won't be needing that."

He nodded at Hunter. The pretty doctor came up behind Walter in her white coat. Walter turned to her. "For your superb service," he said and gave her the flower. Then he looked at Hunter and said shortly, "Shall we go?"

Before Hunter could reply, Walter went through the door and walked outside. The Englishman looked dreamily at the doctor and smiled.

"What is it now, lovebird?" interrupted Walter. He had turned back and was sticking his head impatiently through the door.

Übung 45: Setzen Sie das richtige Pronomen ein!
(me, you, him, her, it, us, them)

1. Walter gave (the nurse) _____ the flower.

2. The dockworker found (Hunter) _____ a job.

3. The children came with (their bicycles) _____.

4. The agents said, "The taxi drivers are following _____."

5. I need to find the tourist office. Can you help _____?

6. Certainly, Sir. I'll show _____ where it is.

7. She stroked the cat and gave _____ some milk.

As they drove into the town, Hunter reported what had happened. At first, Walter complained angrily about the ageing car that Hunter had acquired. Then he realised its advantage: they would not stand out with this car. It looked just like all the other cars on the island.

Walter already knew about the births of deformed children and other mysterious illnesses which had recently affected the people who had been evacuated from the two neighbouring islands. Mary had handled some cases. However, there were Government officials who always took away the patients before the hospital doctors could carry out in-depth examinations.

"So she's called Mary," Hunter noted silently to himself.

Walter was looking at himself through the window in the wing mirror. He adjusted his baseball cap, turning it slightly to one side. The grinning Red Indian, the logo of the 'Cleveland Indians', was now exactly over the middle of his forehead.

"What's your team then?" he asked Hunter.

Hunter thought of the blue and yellow scarf which his mother had given to him when he was at school. "'Chelsea Football Club," he said. Walter immediately drew his colleague from London into a detailed discussion. He had always wondered why two English-speaking nations had the same name for two completely different sports.

While Walter talked animatedly about the origin and meaning of the words 'soccer' and 'football', Hunter concentrated on the road. The road along the cliff top was narrow. The tarmac was full of potholes. Hunter had no desire to share the fate of his pursuers from the day before. He preferred being above water, not under it, and certainly not in a car ….

In the meantime, Walter had moved on to other differences. He was talking about baseball and cricket. Hunter had managed to make some sense of his colleague's explanations of soccer and football, but now, listening with only half an ear, he could not understand a word Walter was saying.

"In principle, both sports use a bat …," explained Walter.

*Übung 46: Übersetzen Sie die Verben! Wann kommt **oneself** hinzu?*

1. sich wehren _____

2. sich verzögern _____

3. sich nähern _____

4. sich entscheiden _____

5. sich befinden _____

6. sich bewaffnen _____

Hunter started signalling. They had come to the crossroads where the coast road led either into the town or to the beach. Walter suddenly stopped speaking. "Stop!" he said. "Signal left. Let's go down to the beach."

Hunter followed Walter's instruction and signalled left. The tarmac road ended and became a gravel path. The path became narrower and narrower and finally ended in a car park. Hunter parked the car. Silently, he cursed his disguise as a Dutch businessman. The jacket of his suit was sticking to his back; his trouser legs were glued to his shins. The car did not have air-conditioning, and in this heat, it made no difference whether the windows were open or shut.

Walter was wearing his light-coloured trekking shorts again, along with sandals and a sleeveless shirt. Hunter bent down and unlaced his shoes. He pulled off his shoes and socks and followed his colleague barefoot. Walter had already reached the beach.

The American threw his shoulder bag onto the sand. He took off his trousers and shirt. Hunter smiled: the Snoopy trunks he was wearing below his trousers looked funny. Feeling Hunter's amused gaze on him, the American said, "Don't stand there grinning, get changed! We've got to talk."

Hunter did not fully understand what the other man meant. Nevertheless, he obeyed the instruction and took off his suit. He did not have any bathing trunks with him. His ordinary boxer shorts, which he was wearing below his long trousers, would have to do. He hurried after Walter into the water.

The American was already standing up to his stomach in the sea. The sun was burning on the surface of the water. Immediately below the surface, the water was lukewarm but deeper down, it was surprisingly cold. Hunter shivered. He splashed around in the gentle waves. The sand gave way under his feet. He took him several moments to reach Walter.

The two men were standing facing each other. The smell of salt tickled Hunter's nose. He thought of Percy, who was probably lying on a packed beach at some club at that very moment. Perhaps he was playing volleyball or learning to surf?

The beach was almost empty. It was early afternoon and, as usual, it was extremely hot. There were a few children playing further along the beach, chasing one another along the sand. Now and again, their cries reached the two men in the water. The only other sound was the gentle rippling noise of the waves.

Übung 47: Markieren Sie mit richtig ✔ oder falsch –!

1. Walter was wearing boots.
2. Hunter was wearing sandals.
3. Walter reached the beach before Hunter.
4. Hunter thought that Walter's shorts look comical.
5. Hunter had brought his swimming trunks with him.
6. Hunter followed Walter into the sea.
7. Hunter found the sea very hot.

"Beautiful, isn't it?" asked the American.

Hunter did not know exactly how to reply. It seemed ridiculous to him to be standing in his shorts in the sea, looking at his colleague. It occurred to him that he really did not know the other man at all. They had not even spent two days together.

"An old agent's trick," the other man began. "No one can eavesdrop on us here."

"An agent never gives away his tips," said Hunter. "No one can eavesdrop on us here, but there's no one to hear us here anyhow."

Tensely, he looked at Walter. From one moment to the next, he was not sure what he thought of the American.

Walker spoke. "We've certainly found out a few things, haven't we? I mean, you and I, we really should put together a plan of what to do next."

Hunter nodded. He wanted to see what the other man had to say. Walter seemed to be thinking the same thing. There was an eager expression on his face too. They looked each other in the eye. Both men were smiling, but their smiles were fixed. Neither man wanted to let his guard down first. Finally, Hunter started to speak. "The Governor is holding a Diplomats' Reception tomorrow night. Mogudi has invited all the big wigs. That would certainly include your Ambassador."

The American's expression did not change. "Yours too." He said. "I mean, you English are very talented when it comes to international relations. A relic of your imperial days?"

Should he take that as a joke? Hunter looked at the other man. He decided to let the comment pass. "Because you work in the Embassy, even if you are undercover, it would be easy for you to get us in, Walter."

"How?" asked the other man.

Hunter splashed his hands around in the waves again. The coldness of the water at his feet was slowly creeping up his legs. He was finding the conversation unpleasant. He explained to Walter what he meant. "As an Embassy employee, you could get us entrance tickets. That's one idea. Or you could smuggle yourself into the Reception with your Ambassador, for example as one of his bodyguards. Or you could be a chauffeur for the evening, or you could … Oh, there are hundreds of possibilities for getting in there." Hunter was slowly becoming impatient. Was he the only one with good ideas?

Walter started splashing his hands through the water as well. His movements were more forceful than Hunter's. He looked at his hands and at the ripples they had made in the water. Without looking up, he said in a calm voice, "Hunter, you're a good man. I could see myself working with you."

Übung 48: Unterstreichen Sie die direkte Rede!

The Englishman hesitated. Surely they were already working with each other? Brenner read the other man's baffled expression correctly. He said, "Listen, I've grown fond of you over the last few days."
"Is that supposed to be a declaration of love?" asked Hunter and laughed awkwardly. His attempt to relax the situation failed.

"I am not undercover in the American Embassy. I am the Ambassador's right-hand man. We've got massive problems with Mogudi. There are major difficulties. The dear chap is not adhering to the contracts."
"Contracts?" repeated Hunter, curiously. "I thought that the Americans were only observing what the Government is doing here. Because American territorial waters are nearby. And because Mogudi and his mates, whoever they are, are involved in underhand transactions, and that's why we're intervening."
Brenner slammed his palms into the water. "For peace, freedom and the benefit of the people?"
"Something like that, yes," agreed Hunter.
"Don't be so naïve! We know exactly what's going on here. Our Government is in it too. Where do you think the Americans are testing their nuclear weapons? Why, here of course!"

Walter spat out the words. All this beating about the bush seemed to be getting too much for him. "So, are you on our side then?"
Hunter stepped backwards. The wet sand on the seabed immediately closed in over his feet. "Wait a minute! Why should I be on your side? You just said that our two countries are on one and the same side, namely, that of the weapons testers."
The feeling that the Walter had simply been sounding him out the whole time made Hunter aggressive. "What's this conversation actually about?" he asked.
"Hunter, are you on our side or not?"
"I'm not on your side at all! What does all this mean, Walter?"
"Then I'm sorry. As I said, you were a good man." The American pulled a waterproof pistol out of his shorts. He held the barrel to Hunter's forehead. "One last chance?" he sneered.

Übung 49: Was bedeuten diese Redewendungen auf Englisch?

1. Um den heißen Brei herumreden
2. Hand und Fuß haben
3. Die Katze aus dem Sack lassen
4. Den Kopf verlieren
5. Seine Finger im Spiel haben
6. Ins Schwarze treffen
7. Jemandem auf den Zahn fühlen

a) ☐ To be exactly correct
b) ☐ To act irrationally
c) ☐ To be well-planned
d) ☐ To be involved in something
e) ☐ To ask somebody lots of questions
f) ☐ To keep away from the subject
g) ☐ To divulge a secret

63

At that moment, Hunter kicked the American in the shins underneath the water. The resistance of the water lessened the blow but his kick was enough to unbalance his attacker. Hunter dived under. He managed to grab hold of his opponent's legs and pulled him below the surface. He pushed him down. Hunter himself wanted to come to the surface for air before he dived under again.

Walter soon took up the fight again. He struck out with his arms and legs. He pushed and pulled at Hunter, who was unable to get to the surface. Hunter held the other man below the waves. He did not have a gun. With the water in his eyes, he could not see where Walter's pistol was. He had no air left. His lungs were burning. He thought they might burst. With his last reserves of energy, he forced himself up, pushing himself from the seabed. His body catapulted to the surface. He gasped for air.

A split second later he was underwater again. The two men wrestled with each other. Walter's heels dug into his stomach and he fell. The American used the opportunity to surface for air. Then the Englishman recovered and pulled him back onto the seabed. Then he noticed that the American's head was in a strange position. Hunter followed his gaze. In the murky waters, he could see a long black object lying in the sand. That must be the gun!

Walter carried on fighting. He released himself from Hunter's grasp and dived to the pistol. Hunter held him firmly by his feet. The other man kicked out. A foot struck Hunter's cheek. The sharp pain made him forget where he was for a moment. His head was throbbing. However, he managed to push himself up from the sand to reach the surface. Gasping for air, he breathed in the sticky summer heat.

Never in his life would Hunter had guessed that Walter was the bad guy. He had even started to like him. Anyway there was no time now for reflecting.

Übung 50: Lesen Sie weiter und setzen Sie die richtigen Präpositionen ein!

Next to him, Walter rose (1.) _____ of the water. "What fun!" he panted. "Hunter, you're a cunning chap. No wonder they put us both (2.) _____ the same team." Walter was juggling the gun (3.) _____ his hands. He twirled it (4.) _____ his finger like a cowboy. Before he could put it away, Hunter grabbed (5.) _____ it. In a flash, the gun was in his hand.

"Hunter, no funny business now!," grinned Walter. "It was a joke. OK? A little joke (6.) _____ friends. A bit of horseplay." Slowly, Hunter aimed the gun (7.) _____ him. Now that he was the target, Walter was nervous. "Don't give me any trouble, man. Put that thing down." Calmly, Hunter kept his gaze fixed (8.) _____ the American.

Without waiting for Hunter's reply, the threatened man added, "Come on Hunter, it was a joke! The gun isn't even loaded. It's a water pistol. Take a closer look at it before you aim it at unarmed colleagues. Do you think that I'd shoot down my own colleague on an international mission? When there are so many stupid people out there in the world who I'd prefer to knock off?"

"Knock off?" repeated Hunter. He thought Walter's words were a strange choice for a man from the Secret Service.

Walter stretched his arm out to him. "Hunter, please give Walter his toy."

Hunter stepped backwards. The other man's arm followed him. With a forceful movement, Walter pushed himself forwards to grab the gun. Hunter started. There was a thud as the bullet came out of the barrel. Walter swayed soundlessly in front of him. His eyes looked at him strangely and then his mouth contorted into an angry "Idiot!"

Blood streamed from the gaping wound in his chest. Hunter saw Walter fall to his knees. His head tipped forward. Then he fell into the water which was fast becoming red around him.

Übung 51: Wie lauten die Substantive im Plural?

1. fisherman

2. tooth

3. beach

4. palm tree

5. berry

6. pair of shorts

Feeling sick, Hunter pushed his way from the spot where Walter had disappeared. Fighting against the resistance of the water, he hurried towards the beach. It was very difficult. With no energy left, he finally reached land. He fell onto the hot sand. He lay there for a few minutes, not moving.

Slowly, life returned to his exhausted body. He had to get away from here. He did not know where he would go, only that he had to get away. With the gun still in his hand, he hurried to his suit, which lay higher up the beach. He gathered together his belongings, collected Walter's clothes and walked quickly to the car.

"What power!" Hunter thought, as his gaze fell on the gun. "For a water pistol!"

Übung 52: Wie lauten die Sätze in der richtigen Reihenfolge?

1. stomach   sick   and   his   was   sore   Hunter   felt.

_____

2. palm   beach   There   trees   along   were   the.

_____

3. green   spiky   the   trees   The   of   leaves   were   and.

_____

4. Their   buried   in   soil   roots   were   the.

_____

5. the   on   sand   Waves   gently   lapped.

_____

Hunter raced the car over the potholes. At the crossroads, he turned his left blinkers on. He wanted to go into the town. He would return to the hotel, change his clothes and think in peace. Then, spontaneously, he turned right. The hotel had not been safe when he had arrived. Why should he return there now?

With the tyres squealing, he went around the bends of the coast road. The need for a shoulder to lean on overpowered him. He had to switch off for a moment. Then he wanted to contact London to clarify what he should do next. Who exactly was it who had got Brenner involved in the operation? This question occupied his mind for several miles. It must have been Mrs Callaghan. So, he realised, his boss still had her fingers in the pie as far as improper weapons transactions were concerned.

Then Hunter realised that it had actually been Captain Martens who had had the idea of multinational co-operation with the US Secret Service. Nevertheless, he thought it was absurd that his immediate superior in the Fifth Rapid Response Troop had a skeleton in his cupboard. He had known the Captain for years. No, he could never believe he was capable of that.
Cooler air flowed through the open car window. The afternoon was turning towards early evening; the heat was dying down. The crunch of the gravel beneath the tyres gave him a welcome feeling of security.
He sat in the car and changed into the linen suit. His boxer shorts were now almost dry.

Übung 53: Unterstreichen Sie das „schwarze Schaf"!

1. brake, wheel, roof, boot, bonnet, funnel
2. think, see, regard, observe, look, inspect
3. on, in, opposite, facing, beside, prior
4. absurd, strange, unusual, normal, peculiar
5. think, ponder, reflect, meditate, manufacture
6. chimney, cupboard, wardrobe, cabinet, bookcase

Hunter had originally wanted to go straight to Mary to tell her about Walter. However, as he entered the reception area of the small hospital, he thought better of it. Confessions and explanations could wait. What he wanted was peace and relaxation, even if only for a few moments. He sat down on one of the wooden chairs opposite the bamboo reception desk and waited. He leafed through some of the glossy magazines laid out on a wobbly table next to him, even though he was not in the right frame of mind for reading. A woman came along the corridor. It was not Mary. A nurse in a white coat with her hair in a ponytail stood in front of him. "Can I help you?" she asked.

"No thank you. I'm waiting for Mary." Hunter opened the magazine again as though he wanted to read it.

"Mary's busy. She's in the operating theatre," explained the young woman helpfully.

"Thank you. I'll wait."

"Do you know Mary?" she wanted to know.

Hunter hesitated before answering. The truth was that he did not know Mary at all. Even so, he had the warm and pleasant feeling of having known her for ever. In his mind's eye, he saw her pretty face. Dreamily, he smiled. The woman drew her own conclusions from his expression and asked, "So you're the famous Walter?"

Hunter quickly took advantage of the opportunity and replied, "Yes, that's me!"

The woman laid her hand warmly on his. "Then Mary certainly won't mind if I take you to her."

Hesitantly, Hunter replaced the magazine on the table. "I thought you said Mary was in an operation?" he inquired.

The nurse laughed. "Yes," she said, "but it won't bother the patient if you go and have a chat with her."

Hunter was very happy to get to know Mary better.

69

! *Übung 54: Schreiben Sie die Zahlen aus!*

1. $^1/_2$ _____

2. 14th _____

3. 2004 _____

4. 1.02 _____

5. 7,000,000 _____

6. $^3/_4$ _____

7. 0.27 _____

The nurse accompanied him to the end of the corridor. Then she knocked on a wooden door and slipped in through the gap. A few moments later, she was standing in front of him again. "You can go in," she winked. "Have fun!"

Hunter entered the room. There was extremely cold air coming from the large fan above him. Mary had her back towards him. Her waist was narrow and she had shapely hips. Her long legs were covered just above the knees by a green coat. He could see her toned calves. His gaze wondered upwards. Her neck was bare. Wisps of hair had escaped from her ponytail. From the movement of her arms, he saw that she was cutting something.

! *Übung 55: Setzen Sie die Question Tags ein!*

1. That's a child, _____?

2. He is kind, _____?

3. They have travelled across the Atlantic, _____?

4. She was cutting something, _____?

5. We were talking together, _____?

6. The doctors will be arriving soon, _____?

7. I need to reassure him, _____?

Hunter cleared his throat. Mary kept her back to him, saying, "Walter, it's so nice that you've come. I'll be finished in a moment. What's the other chap doing, the Englishman?"

Hunter mumbled something.

"Have you converted him yet?" she asked cheerfully. "I still think you should leave the matter alone" She stopped for a moment. "That's disgusting," she said to herself. Speaking over her shoulder, she said loudly, "Can you just get me one of those glass plates? They're next to the microscope."

Hunter mumbled again, this time in agreement. He took one of the glass plates from the rack. He stayed behind her as he reached it to her. She touched his fingers as she took the glass. A quiver went through him. She giggled. Then, with the plate in one hand and the scalpel in the other, she turned around. She saw Hunter and, shocked, said, "You're …"

He helped her. "I'm Hunter, Walter's colleague." She kept looking at him and did not seem to have understood. Hunter added, "The Englishman." He understood her silence to be embarrassment. To help her get over it, he stood next to her and asked, "What are you doing then?"

"No!" she said as she waved him away.

"That doesn't bother me," said Hunter coolly. She had been cutting up a corpse. The green sheet which lay over the dead body had a square hole and there were clips holding the skin apart below the hole. The person's organs were clearly visible.

Hunter choked. However, he wanted to impress Mary, and so did not allow himself to be deterred by a second "No!" He bent over the sheet and studied the intestines. Before the doctor could pull him away from the bed, he raised the end of the sheet covering the corpse's head.

The agent gasped. He was still in shock as the doctor took the sheet out of his hand and replaced it over the person's face.

"I told you," she complained.

Hunter muttered. "That's unbelievable. That's horrendous."

Her answer was sober. "We're working on it."

He had seen many things in his work as an agent, but what he had seen below the sheet beat everything. "That's a child, isn't it? Or what is it?" His voice trembled.

Übung 56: Bilden Sie sinnvolle Wörter!

Carefully, he dared to look at the (1. rcdoeve) _____ body again. Only then did he realise that the (2. scpoer) _____ was not particularly big. The (3. dclhi) _____ must have only been two or, at the most, three years old. He had no face. In the place of his eyes, there was only skin and the child's nose and mouth (4. dfeomr) _____ an ugly harelip with nothing to (5. aseertpa) _____ them.

"You're right. That child has slipped (6. tghhruo) _____ the Government's (7. rfeisng) _____. He's one of them who caught it right at the beginning.

During the second period of testing, the people from the Health Department were much more thorough. As far as I know, they killed all of them as soon as they were born." Mary suddenly stopped speaking. "Let's go," she said.

"What, all of them? What do you mean by 'them'?" Hunter was not about to let the matter drop. Confused, she looked at him, "Walter said you were a colleague. One of us, I thought."
The agent's "Yes" came a little too slowly. She turned her head suspiciously. "Or aren't you?" she asked.
Hunter did not care anymore. The dead child whom she had been dealing with was too much. So that was what Lily had been speaking about. The children from the areas exposed to radiation. The children whose mothers came from the other two islands.
"So there *was* weapons testing two years ago as well, wasn't there? And now? More testing?" His words echoed around the room. In the quietness that followed, the only thing that could be heard was the rhythmical whirring of the fan.

Übung 57: Übersetzen Sie folgende Sätze ins Englische!

1. Wenn wir Zeit hätten, könnten wir es herausfinden.

_____

2. Wenn ich mehr Geld hätte, könnte ich einen Ausflug machen.

_____

3. Wenn sie nett wäre, würde ich sie mögen.

_____

"Why is the child dead?"

She shrugged. "Would you like to live like that?"

Hunter stared at the doctor. "*Would* you like to live like that or *could* you live like that?"

"Lots of people *can* live," she retorted weakly. "Do you think I like doing that job?"

Hunter was stunned. Her? This woman whom he had been dreaming of since their very first meeting? "You're a murderer!" he bellowed at her.

She stood firm against his attack. "No," she said. "I'm just helping to straighten things out where people's curiosity has got out of hand. And now you can get out."

"I won't. Give me the names of the people who are making you do this!" Hunter challenged her to a confession. He knew that she would confess. Whatever had brought her into the clutches of these criminals who had such contempt for humanity, it must have been against her will.

Übung 58: Setzen Sie passende Fragewörter ein!

1. "_____ did you get in?" Antwort: "Through the window."

2. "_____ did the nurse let you in?" Antwort: "At 10.00 a.m."

3. "_____ are you so angry?" Antwort: "Because he's so stupid!"

4. "_____ did you find out about it?" Antwort: "I read the newspaper."

5. "_____ can we see the patient?" Antwort: "This evening."

"Where is Walter?" she asked. "You've come to me without Walter! Why?" Red blotches appeared on her cheeks and she gasped, "You've killed Walter, haven't you? Haven't you?" Mary was shouting loudly. "Where is he?"

The agent's answer was cool and distant. "Walter is dead, Mary."

With a horrified "No!," she threw herself towards him. She shouted the word again and again. She hit him repeatedly with her left hand. He tried to grab her wrist to stop her, but her anger and grief gave her almost superhuman strength. She stopped for a fraction of a second. She was looking at her right fist which she had not yet raised towards Hunter. The scalpel in her hand glittered in the dying light coming through the window. She rammed it deep into Hunter's thigh. Before she could twist it around to cause serious injury to his leg, he seized her by the shoulders.

He pushed her violently away from him. She fell backwards against the wall. Her bones snapped and her body slipped lifelessly to the floor. She was sitting upright against the wall. Her eyes stared into the distance. A thin thread of blood slowly ran out of the corner of her mouth. She still held the scalpel in her hand.

Übung 59: Welcher Satz enthält die richtige Zeitform?

1. Sie haben Walter umgebracht.
   a) ☐ You will kill Walter.
   b) ☐ You are going to kill Walter.
   c) ☐ You have killed Walter.

2. Die Frau warf sich auf ihn.
   a) ☐ The woman threw herself towards him.
   b) ☐ The woman is throwing herself towards him.
   c) ☐ The woman had thrown herself towards him.

3. Ich habe es Ihnen schon gegeben.
   a) ☐ I had already given it to you.
   b) ☐ I was already giving it to you.
   c) ☐ I have already given it to you.

Hunter hurried to the doctor. He felt for her pulse, but there was none. Her neck must have broken when she hit the wall. He took his fingers away from her neck and looked at her. The scalpel fell from her lifeless hand with a tinkling noise. Her head fell to her chest and she tipped sidewards. Hunter intercepted her fall. Carefully, he laid the dead body on the floor. He felt nothing.

Suddenly, he heard loud footsteps coming along the corridor in front of the room. There were several people running towards the operating theatre. Quickly, he looked around for a hiding place, but the sparse furnishings of the room did not provide any cover. He sprinted to the open window and jumped out. A flowerbed cushioned his fall. He rolled over swiftly and stood up. He hesitated for a second and then ducked into the shadows of a house wall and ran towards the car park.

Übung 60: Unterstreichen Sie das passende Wort!

1. He felt for her pulse/heartbeat.
2. She was dissecting the corpse with a scalpel/razor.
3. The heat was impenetrable/unbearable.
4. The flies were swarming around/milling around.
5. They were exploring/examining the x-rays.
6. He was lying in the shade/shadows.
7. The island was sparsely/spartanly populated.

Hunter's car had disappeared. The car park was now completely empty. The agent was not surprised. He now expected things like that to happen.

"Surely there's a garage or somewhere for the staff to park," thought Hunter. Shielded by the building wall, he retraced his steps. Then he heard raised voices coming from the back of the building. He could not understand exactly what the people were saying. Because he did not have his gun with him, he decided to avoid further confrontation with surgical instruments.

The scalpel wound was a little painful. A crust had formed almost all the way around the injury to his thigh and it stemmed the flow of blood. The light material of his trousers stuck to the wound. Hunter knew that it would be incredibly sore when he took off his trousers. Nevertheless, because he did not have any bandages, he was glad that the injury was looking after itself.

He ran quietly over the grass to the huts which were located at one side of the garden. Most of the windows were covered. There was light behind the thick curtains of many of the huts. People's shadows moved behind them. The first two wooden cabins seemed to be empty. Hunter crept around the front hut. There were about ten huts in total. Their entrances all faced away from the garden. A gravel path linked the doors.

Übung 61: Unterstreichen Sie die Adjektive im Text!

Beyond the path there was a tall fence which blocked the way into the neighbouring forest. It was a thick jungle. In the dusky evening light, the agent could see a tangle of lush plants stretching up into the sky. The loud bird noises sounded alien to him. Still, this was not the time to be enjoying the exotic paradise. He could not allow himself to get distracted by his tropical surroundings.

Hunter continued to make his way along the wooden walls. When he came to the first lit window, he stopped. Here, too, the thick curtains were drawn. However, one corner of the material was flapping in the light breeze. Hunter realised that the window behind it was open. He crept closer. With one finger, he lifted the heavy, dark material. Carefully, so as not to make any noise, he crept even closer. He peered through the gap. He gasped. For a second, he was routed to the spot. What he saw was horrific. "Not again!" he thought to himself. There were several cots lined up in the room and with sleeping children in them. A nurse in a white coat was cradling one of the children in her arm. The child was no more than a few months old. Hunter could see directly over the woman's shoulder. The baby's small face was the same as that of the dead child in the operating theatre.

That was enough for him. He was physically and mentally exhausted. Stumbling, he felt his way back along the wooden walls. He did not care about a car anymore. He did not want to find a garage. He only wanted to get away. "Even if I've got to walk the whole way!" he thought to himself.

! *Übung 62: Setzen Sie die richtige Konjunktion ein!*
(and, or, if/when, unless, while)

1. You cannot work as an agent _____ you are very clever.

2. You will be sent on an assignment _____ you qualify.

3. You must sit some examinations _____ you are training.

4. You must hold a British passport _____ a driving licence.

5. To apply, you must be aged 40 _____ under.

Hunter walked towards the town, setting one foot in front of the other. He was extremely tired. He kept walking. While he was still in the vicinity of the Foreign Aid Centre, every time that a car approached, he hid himself in the bushes at the side of the road. There was too great a risk that he would be seen by one of Mary's colleagues or that somebody would pursue him.

More than an hour later, as darkness was beginning to fall, Hunter decided to stop one of the passing vehicles. The coast road was quiet in the evening, and it was some time before another vehicle approached. Hunter put out his arm to thumb a lift. A rather shabby lorry stopped. There were fruit boxes stacked on the loading area and they flew around dramatically as the vehicle came to a sudden stop. As far as Hunter could tell, the driver was not at all worried about his freight.

Übung 63: Formulieren Sie die Sätze im Aktiv!

1. The car was overtaken by the lorry.

_____

2. Hunter was arrested by a policeman.

_____

3. The oranges were picked by the women.

_____

4. The fruit crates were packed by the workers.

_____

5. The instruction was given by Hunter's colleague.

_____

The lorry driver had friendly eyes and a dark face. He looked cheerfully at the agent. Hunter climbed in and they drove into the town. He told the helpful driver that he was a tourist here and had lost his way. The other man did not ask him any questions, preferring to talk about the interesting sights on the island. Hunter found the same openness and friendliness in the driver as he had experienced at Lily's house.

Suddenly, it was clear to Hunter what he should do. He would collect his belongings from the hotel and ask Lily to put him up. He had to pay for the stolen car somehow. Or, better still: the Secret Service had to pay. In any case, he needed a car for his assignment.

Übung 64: Enträtseln Sie das Lösungswort!

1. Money used in a country _ _ _ _ □ _ _ _

2. To interrogate someone
   is to ask … □ _ _ _ _ _ _ _ _

3. Camouflage or incognito _ _ _ _ □ _ _ _

4. Walkie-talkie _ _ _ □ _

5. Device for transmitting speech _ _ _ _ □ _ _ _

6. Electronic data processor _ _ □ _ _ _ _

7. Book describing a country _ _ _ _ □ _ _ _

8. Eyewear with dark lenses _ _ □ _ _ _ _ _ _

9. Small battery-powered lamp □ _ _ _ _

Lösung: _ _ _ _ _ _ _ _ _

The lorry driver dismissed the agent's objections and drove him right up to the hotel door. When he saw the dilapidated building, he looked at Hunter sympathetically. Hunter got out of the lorry. The crates on the loading area rumbled as the vehicle moved away.

The porter was nowhere to be seen as Hunter walked towards the desk. He pressed the old-fashioned bell and waited. No one came. He collected his key from the board behind the desk himself. He really would have to have a serious word with the people in London. Who had found this hotel for him?

He looked at the clock to check the time. The time difference between the two zones was eight hours. That meant he could use his mobile to give his situation report to London without waking up anyone there. "Never wake a colleague on the night shift," he chuckled to himself.

As he turned the key in the lock of his room door, Hunter noticed that it was open. He was totally sure that he had locked the door behind him when he had left the room that morning.

Übung 65: Sind die folgenden Sätze richtig ✔ oder falsch –?

1. The fire extinguisher is in a cupboard.
2. Hunter cannot reach the fire extinguisher.
3. Hunter tries to find out of there is anyone in the room before he goes in.
4. He hears a quiet throbbing noise.
5. The book makes a noise as it falls.
6. Hunter sets off the fire extinguisher.

The agent looked around the corridor. What could he use as a weapon? A fire extinguisher hung on the wall near the stairs.

Hunter lifted it out of its holder and returned to his room. He listened at the door, but could not hear anything inside. With a sudden movement, he pushed open the door and jumped into the room.

There was a small thump as the book leaning against the door fell. Hunter aimed the hose of the fire extinguisher into the room, ready to set it off. There was no one to be seen. The wire which he had stretched across the room as a trip wire had disappeared. In its place was a sports bag, which stood next to the bed.

Looking around carefully, the agent approached the bag. He listened, but again there was nothing to be heard. No ticking bomb, nothing. He put the fire extinguisher down on the carpet. Slowly, he opened the zip of the bag. There was something red inside.

*Übung 66: Setzen Sie die richtige Zeitform des Verbs **to see** ein!*

1. I _____ him every day.
2. I _____ just _____ him.
3. I _____ him yesterday.
4. I _____ _____ him now.
5. I _____ already _____ him that morning.
6. I _____ _____ _____ him tomorrow.

"Aha!" A shout came from the bathroom. Hunter turned, grabbed the fire extinguisher and aimed at the door to the adjoining room. A gawky man stood on the threshold. He was over six foot tall and had brown eyes and brown hair. His thin legs were visible below brightly-coloured, baggy shorts. His arms poked out of a white T-shirt with a cartoon drawing on it.

"Other countries, other customs, is that what you mean?" asked the young man and pointed at the fire extinguisher.

Hunter could only say, "Horn! What are you doing here then?"

Hunter's assistant smiled. "Surprise! I thought that you might need some help!"

Übung 67: Bilden Sie Genitivkonstruktionen und setzen Sie den Apostroph an der richtigen Stelle ein!

1. The sports bag belonging to the man.

2. The flag of the country.

3. The customs of the country.

4. The suitcases belonging to the tourists.

5. The equipment brought by the agents.

6. The progress made by his colleague.

Hunter did not understand why his assistant from the London Secret Service Headquarters was standing there in front of him. Percy saw that further explanations were needed. "The holiday thing in the club was all very well, but I'm not one for shows. Mind you, you should have seen me in the musical, 'Saturday Night Fever'; I dare say I wasn't the worst singer!"

Hunter looked at him in astonishment.

"In a word," resumed Horn, "it was too boring for me there. So because I wasn't far from you, I took the next plane and whizzed over. How's the case going? What are we doing?"

Übung 68: Bilden Sie sinnvolle Wörter!

1. The (qrseeHautdar) _____ of the Secret Service was in London.

2. To provide an explanation is to provide (orflicniaiact) _____.

3. Someone who is astonished is (dsuperirs) _____.

4. Madonna is a (rpaopst) _____.

5. She is very (cmisula) _____. She sings very well.

6. Opera and theatre are forms of (tmenanitrtene) _____.

7. The (lreopaena) _____ landed at the airport.

Hunter made the obligatory call to London. He described the recent events to Captain Martens in detail. Percy listened with his mouth open while his boss spoke on his mobile telephone. The young man was only just beginning his career as an agent and had scarcely had any experience in external duty. Martens did not allow Hunter to exchange his hotel room for private accommodation. Even when the agent explained the advantages of staying at Lily's house to the

Director of the Rapid Response Troop again, the Captain remained firm.

Meanwhile, the British Foreign Minister and the British Diplomat who was on the same island as Hunter had received death threats. The French and the Spanish secret services had also reported that their Foreign Ministers and Ambassadors despatched to the island state had received threats. It remained unclear who was behind it all. Experts in London were still examining the letters containing the threats. From the writing and the vocabulary, they were probably written by Russians.

Übung 69: Setzen Sie die richtigen Reflexivpronomen ein!

1. He washes _____.

2. They have just washed _____.

3. We washed _____ yesterday.

4. She is washing _____ now.

5. Have you already washed _____?

6. The cat was sitting in the sun, washing _____.

7. I will wash _____ tomorrow.

"What do these people want with their threats?" enquired Hunter. The Captain admitted openly that he did not know. "I think it's all very strange. The letters say that the Ministers and the Ambassadors should leave. Two of them are already as good as destroyed. Our politicians should keep out of the whole matter; otherwise the other two will be contaminated. Funny, isn't it? Can you make any sense of it?"

Hunter kept his suspicions to himself. He had an idea what the letters meant, but only a very vague one.

Übung 70: Bilden Sie Wortfamilien!

das Adjektiv: thoughtful

1. der Komparativ: _____

2. der Superlativ: _____

3. das Adverb: _____

4. das Substantiv: _____

das Adjektiv: good

1. der Komparativ: _____

2. der Superlativ: _____

3. das Adverb: _____

4. das Substantiv: _____

Hunter had explained the situation in detail to Percy Horn the previous evening. The young man did not have Walter's relaxed and professional manner, but there was no danger that he would murder Hunter. That point was definitely in Horn's favour.

While his assistant said that he would obtain a new car for Lily, Hunter made his way to the harbour. He had put on the blue overalls and knitted hat again. They made him very hot. However, he realised that he had no other choice if he did not want to stand out among the dockworkers.

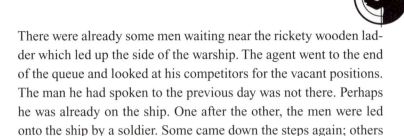

There were already some men waiting near the rickety wooden ladder which led up the side of the warship. The agent went to the end of the queue and looked at his competitors for the vacant positions. The man he had spoken to the previous day was not there. Perhaps he was already on the ship. One after the other, the men were led onto the ship by a soldier. Some came down the steps again; others did not reappear.

The Argentinians did not seem to be taking much time for each interview as everything went very quickly. After a quarter of an hour, it was Hunter's turn. He followed the soldier onto the deck and was shown into the Captain's cabin. The room was furnished like an office. The walls were decorated by all kinds of nautical objects.

Hunter sat down on a heavy brown leather chair. The Captain of the ship sat opposite him in his dark-blue naval uniform. Hunter impressed him with his knowledge of the Spanish language. The Argentinian was pleased, saying that at least he would have somebody in the engine room who understood his commands.

Hunter signed a contract for ten days. It was for a 'trial manoeuvre', as the Captain described it. A type of operation during which the ship would be thoroughly tested. For the operation, he needed able seamen to work in the engine room and the stores alongside the soldiers.

Übung 71: Lesen Sie weiter und beantworten Sie folgende Fragen zum Text!

1. What does Hunter want to ask a question about?

_____

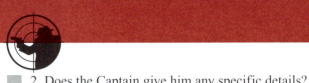

2. Does the Captain give him any specific details?

3. What is the soldier wearing?

4. Do we find out exactly how many men are already in the galley?

5. Are the men talking loudly or quietly?

6. What are the three men in the corner talking about?

"You'll find out later exactly what you have to do." The Captain concluded the interview before Hunter could ask anything about his duties. Another soldier dressed in camouflage led Hunter to the galley. There were already several men sitting there. Hunter had seen some of them in the queue on the quay. The man from yesterday was not there yet. The men's conversations were subdued. Because no one knew what would happen during the next ten days, some of the men were making wild speculations. Others were silent. In one corner, three men were talking about the ship's size, speed and loading capacity. Hunter listened but soon realised that they did not exactly know what they were talking about and were only making assumptions.

There was coffee to drink and dry biscuits to eat. Slowly, the room filled. A man waved as he came in. It was the friendly man from the previous day. As there were no seats free next to Hunter, he sat down at a different table. He kept looking over at Hunter, winking or giving the thumbs-up in a gesture which meant, "We've made it, we're on!" Hunter made the V-sign with his index and middle finger.

An officer entered the room. He told the group to follow him. After a tour of the ship, they all had time to fetch their belongings. The ship would sail at around 10.00 p.m.

Übung 72: Schreiben Sie Zahlen statt Worte auf!

1. One point five _____

2. Thirty thousand _____

3. Nineteen eighty four _____

4. Five eighths _____

5. Zero point five four _____

Hunter followed the group down the steel staircase into the engine room. Here it was even hotter and stickier than it was outside. Enthusiastically, some of the men questioned the officer. They even stroked the pumps and machinery furtively. The three men who had been talking shop earlier whispered excitedly while the officer described the work area and the tasks to be carried out. Hunter fell behind as the group with the uniformed soldier moved on into the next area of the engine room. He hid behind a switch box on the wall of the ship until there was enough distance between him and the other men. Then he turned around and crept back to the stairs.

The stairs led down even further into the bowels of the ship. Hunter did not have to search for long. There was only one steel door here. It was secured with a combination lock. Hunter had borrowed a metal box with a small pin from Percy's luggage. He inserted the pin into the lock. Hunter waited a few moments until the whirring figures on the digital display had found the code. The lock snapped open.

Übung 73: Unterstreichen Sie die Hauptsätze!

With a huge effort, he prized open the heavy metal door. Behind it there was a long corridor, which was lit by dim ceiling lights. The agent closed the door and walked forwards. In comparison to the engine room a deck higher, here it was considerably cooler. A few metres away from the door, there were some wooden boxes with heavy iron hinges. Using the short crowbar which he pulled out of his trouser pocket, Hunter lifted the lid of one of the boxes. It contained wood-wool. There were machine guns buried in the wool.

The next box which he opened contained a whole consignment of hand grenades. In contrast to the guns, which seemed to be several years old, the grenades were relatively new. As far as Hunter could tell, they were not American products. The next box was disappointing: its contents were very new. It contained short-barrel guns, which seemed to have come from old Russian Army stocks.
Hunter put the crowbar away. He was on a warship and he had found weapons. That was not the reason he had smuggled himself in as a worker. He could have guessed that he would have found guns on a warship.

Übung 74: Welches Satzzeichen ist gemeint? Ordnen Sie zu!

1. Exclamation mark
2. Full stop
3. Brackets
4. Semi-colon
5. Hyphen
6. Question mark
7. Colon
8. Comma
9. Asterisk
10. Apostrophe
11. Quotation marks

a) ☐ .
b) ☐ ?
c) ☐ " "
d) ☐ ,
e) ☐ *
f) ☐ !
g) ☐ '
h) ☐ ( )
i) ☐ ;
j) ☐ :
k) ☐ -

Hunter continued along the corridor. High metal trunks took the place of the wooden crates. Behind them there were boxes which, according to their labels, contained torpedoes. To check that the boxes did actually contain torpedoes, the agent opened the lock of one of them. A torpedo approximately one metre in length lay before him, wrapped in protective wood-wool. There was an attachment on the upper side of the weapon. It was marked with the symbol for radioactivity. Hunter could see that the attachment was a lead cartridge under which there was enriched plutonium. He removed the small container without difficulty.

"So Lily was right!" he thought.

"Hey! What are you doing?"

Hunter jumped. Thinking quickly, he hid the cartridge in his trouser pocket. He had not heard the man approaching from behind. A soldier almost six foot tall stood in front of him in the corridor, aiming his machine gun towards him. His khaki uniform and heavy black combat boots made him look even taller and broader than he was. Hunter immediately decided to forget everything he knew of the Spanish language. In broken Creole, he stuttered that he had lost the rest of the party.

"What a shame for you," said the other man harshly. "That means you've lost your job here before even starting." A throaty laugh came from his mouth and echoed unpleasantly loudly on the metal of the ship's walls.

Übung 75: Setzen Sie die passenden Negativformen ein! (no, never, nothing, nowhere, no one)

1. There was _____ in the torpedo chamber.

2. There were _____ bullets in the guns.

3. The agent had _____ killed anybody.

4. _____ was walking on the deck.

5. Hunter saw _____ soldiers.

6. The soldiers were _____ to be seen.

The agent took advantage of the moment. He ducked down, giving the soldier a hard kick in the knee. The soldier shouted in pain as his kneecap dislocated. The agent grabbed the barrel of the machine gun and pulled at it. His opponent held on tightly to the gun. The two men wrestled for the weapon.

Then, with his elbow, the soldier gave Hunter a heavy blow to his chin. Hunter saw stars for a moment but recovered quickly. He raised his knee and kicked the soldier in the stomach. The other man gasped but still he kept hold of the weapon. Some shots were set off. The bullets bounced noisily against the wall of the ship. Some embedded themselves in the metal, but others were slung back. The soldier won the upper hand. He slammed his massive fist into the agent's chest. Hunter stumbled backwards and fell. Before a volley of shots could reach him, he slid nimbly to one side. He squatted down behind the box with the torpedo. However, he knew that this hiding place was anything but safe.

Übung 76: Setzen Sie ein!
(up, down, in, out)

1. To bring _____ the Government.

2. To work _____ the solution.

3. To bring _____ the washing.

4. To add _____ the figures.

5. To note _____ a telephone number.

6. To give _____ to a difficulty.

7. To find _____ the answer.

The man in the khaki uniform fired above the crate in order to hit Hunter. Hunter kept still. The solder walked towards the torpedo while he spoke into his radio to request help. He was moving closer. When he was close enough to the crate, Hunter jumped up. He pushed the metal box forwards. The corner of the box slammed violently into the soldier's injured knee. He cried out in pain. His radio slipped out of his hand. Hunter's hand closed around the barrel of the machine gun. The soldier pressed the trigger. Shots were fired against the ship's walls and the boxes. Hunter twisted his arm to one side, and the shots now fired down the corridor towards the door. He could hear footsteps coming down the stairs. They were getting louder. Hunter pushed the heel of his boot into his opponent's knee. The man howled. His gun went off again.

*Übung 77: Setzen Sie **could, would** oder **should** ein!*

1. He _____ hear footsteps coming along the corridor.
2. You _____ telephone him. He might be unwell.
3. I _____ obey the command if I were you!
4. The soldiers _____ see the men fighting.
5. Don't damage that box! There _____ be ammunition inside!

With a cracking noise, the shots hit one of the wooden boxes. For a moment, the footsteps and voices which had reached the door were silent. Then the ammunition in the box ignited in hundreds of small explosions. The men screamed and somebody yelled, "Retreat!"
The men started pounding back up the staircase. The soldier with whom Hunter had been fighting finally tired when he heard his comrades escaping from the hissing and crackling of the explosions. Hunter tore his gun away from him. He used the butt of the weapon to give the solder a heavy blow to his temple. The man fell unconscious to the floor.
The fire was spreading in the corridor in front of the agent. The wooden crates and the wood-wool were burning like tinder. The flames had reached other ammunition boxes and this caused more

explosions. The ship's walls were trembling. One of the explosions had torn a gaping hole in the side of the vessel. Hunter saw how the metal at the edges of the hole was bulging inwards. Then he took a deep breath and raced through the flames. He felt the intense heat which threatened to singe his skin. He reached the door and leapt towards the staircase.

Übung 78: Bilden Sie den Imperativ!
Beispiel: You must go home. Go home!

1. You must stop fighting.

_____

2. Please could you open the window?

_____

3. You should stop now!

_____

4. Please would you evacuate the ship!

_____

5. You must start the engine.

_____

6. I want you to leave it there.

_____

7. You must help me.

_____

The water started gushing through the hole in the ship's hull. It engulfed the fire and swept into the ship. The force of the water made Hunter lose his grip. He fell. The water closed over his head. The agent thrashed about. He pushed himself up off the ground and managed to grab hold of the stair rail. He gasped for air, breathing heavily. He raced frantically up the stairs. The water behind him was rising. Now that it was spreading out through the lower deck, the water had less force. Hunter arrived on the next deck where the news of the hole and the flooding had already been received.

The shrill noise of an alarm sounded from the bridge. The men were running; commands echoed through the passageways. There was no hope of an orderly evacuation.

The chaos on the upper decks was increasing. There was frantic hustle and bustle at the top of the stairs leading onto the open deck. The soldiers were all pushing past one another. A voice could be heard on a loudspeaker, ordering the soldiers to launch the lifeboats into the water. However, the lifeboats were of no use on this side, as the ship was berthed at the dock. Nevertheless, some of the crew tried to save themselves by releasing the lifeboats onto the dock and sliding down ropes into them.

Übung 79: Unterstreichen Sie das „schwarze Schaf"!

1. gush, surge, stream, feel, run
2. hull, bridge, tyre, bows, funnel, sails
3. pant, wheeze, gasp, breathe, blow, murmur
4. weakness, force, strength, power, energy
5. hole, blockage, gap, crevice, opening, puncture
6. deep, shrill, loud, soft, happy, low

With a heavy jolt, the ship sank several metres deeper. "The Titanic took longer than this to go down," thought Hunter to himself grimly. He pushed his way through the soldiers, who were fighting chaotically. The officers and the Captain were shouting through the windows of the bridge, trying in vain to restore order to the crew.

Finally, Hunter reached the open deck. The ship shuddered again. With a loud cracking noise, a section of the stern broke away from the rest of the vessel. The rear part of the ship sank beneath the waves. Some of the men shouted out as they lost their footing and fell into the water. Hunter fought on until he reached the bow. He climbed onto the railing and pushed himself off with both legs. With his arms stretched out in front of him, he dived into the sea. He entered the water gracefully, disappeared for a few seconds and then came back to the surface. Using a front crawl stroke, he swam quickly away from the ship, past the furthermost docks and to the very end of the dock area. The waves were not very strong but his destination was a long way away.

The chaos behind him grew quieter. Hunter continued to fight his way through the water. When he came to the last dock, he heaved himself up. He lay on the hot concrete. The sun burned onto his exhausted body. The only thing he wanted to do was sleep.

*Übung 80: Schreiben Sie die Sätze im will-Future! Beenden Sie jeden Satz mit **tomorrow**!*
Beispiel: I swam 1,000 metres yesterday. I will swim 1,000 metres tomorrow.

1. They ran a mile yesterday.

2. You cycled 20 miles yesterday.

_____

3. We played one match yesterday.

_____

4. He won three games yesterday.

_____

5. She watched five hours of tennis yesterday.

_____

Hunter's lips were dry and his head throbbed. His limbs felt like lead. He had no idea how long he had been lying on the dock beneath the scorching sun. Slowly, he pulled himself up.

In the distance, he saw the hull of the Argentinian warship protruding out of the water. The seabed in the harbour was not far below the surface. A huge steel structure like the warship would not disappear completely below the water. Hunter could see crowds of people milling around the ship's berth. Ambulances stood at the entrance to the dock. Police vehicles, with their blue lights flashing noiselessly, blocked the road from the dock entrance.

Hunter was dizzy as he walked towards the first docks. He had sunstroke. His stomach grumbled; he was hungry. He wanted to telephone Percy and ask his colleague to pick him up. However, the mobile telephone in his trouser pocket had not survived its dip in the cold water. There was nothing Hunter could do but keep walking.

He had no desire to return to the scene of destruction. Instead, at the end of the dock, he turned to a wall. He still had enough strength to climb up and over the wall. Gracefully, he jumped down

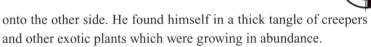

onto the other side. He found himself in a thick tangle of creepers and other exotic plants which were growing in abundance.

Hunter sighed; he was exhausted. Carefully, he picked his way through the jungle. It was not long before the sweat began to drip from his forehead.

Übung 81: Wie lauten die Sätze in der richtigen Reihenfolge?

1. people   to   hospital   Ambulances   take   injured.

___

2. cars   Police   lights   which   blue   flash   have.

___

3. are   red   normally   engines   Fire.

___

4. Trucheons   are   carried   by   weapons   policemen.

___

5. receive   training   Ambulance   special   drivers.

___

6. The   loud   make   a   noise   sirens.

___

Back in the hotel, Hunter took a long shower. The warm water soothed his aching muscles. The wound on his thigh was now barely visible. When he had finished, he put on his dressing gown and

99

lay down on the bed. He rested to regain his strength. His stomach grumbled again, but Hunter could not manage to get up to go and find something to eat.

It was already dusky when Hunter woke up. The fan above his bed was switched off. There was no light in the room and it was stuffy. Hunter saw a strip of light underneath the bathroom door. He went over and knocked.

Percy was drying his hair with a towel and indicated to Hunter that he could come in. Hunter sat down on the side of the bath. While Percy continued to rub the hand towel over his hair, his boss summarised the events at the docks. Suddenly, Hunter remembered, "The cartridge!"

His assistant threw the towel onto a hook on the wall. Calmly, he said, "Don't worry; I rescued it from your pocket." He pointed at the tooth mugs near the washbasin. The lead container was in one of them. Hunter sighed with relief.

Percy looked happily at his boss. At last, he was on a proper mission. His work would continue that evening. The Diplomats' Reception at the Governor's villa was on the agenda.

"We've been invited to dinner," announced the junior agent. "There'll only be canapés at the Reception, so I thought I'd accept Lily's offer for us both. That woman is great! Her husband wasn't at home, but she thinks that he'll like the new car too."

Übung 82: Unterstreichen Sie die richtige Präsensform!

1. Percy and Hunter are getting ready/get ready for the Reception.
2. The men are talking/talk while they decide what to do.
3. Every evening, Hunter has/is having a shower.
4. Tonight, he is enjoying/enjoys a bath.

5. Then he changes/is changing into his smart black suit.
6. He is looking forward/looks forward to finding out more information.
7. Percy brushes/is brushing his hair in front of the mirror.

Hunter himself did not feel like going visiting before the Reception. However, the meal at Lily's house was not only enjoyable and entertaining, but it also gave Hunter and Percy some new information for their mission later that evening.

After the hostess's sister had gathered all the children to send them to bed, the remaining adults talked about the previous days' events. Hunter listened thoughtfully to Lily's report on the demonstration that had taken place that morning. It had been broken up by even greater use of violence than the last time. The agent knew he did not have to mince his words with Lily and her husband. He told them of his grotesque discoveries at the Foreign Aid Centre and of the weapons he had found on the warship. His audience was hardly surprised: Hunter was only confirming what they had already thought.

Lily's husband was a quick-witted and intelligent man of about forty. He explained how, two years previously, Mogudi's Government had sold other nations the right to carry out nuclear weapons testing in the islands. The consequences had been devastating. The international community had cautioned Mogudi. He had claimed to know nothing of the whole matter. The countries which had tested their weapons also declared themselves innocent. Some people were punished, but those who were said to be responsible were always individuals.

During recent months, more and more warships with foreign flags had sailed into the town's harbour. Mysterious incidents were increasing. Lily's husband added to Lily's tales of dead fishermen, the evacuation of the two neighbouring islands and the births of the disfigured children.

"I would love to do more than just demonstrate and write letters to international newspapers which no one prints," he said. Hunter listened. He had an idea.

*Übung 83: Setzen Sie die richtige Zeitform von **to have** ein!*

Lily's husband sighed. He (1.) _____ a long day. He (2.) _____ a headache and a sore back. He (3.) _____ problems sleeping because his back was so sore. However, he had to keep working as the family was poor and (4.) _____ no money. He told himself that they (5.) _____ a holiday in the summer once they (6.) _____ more money. "We (7.) _____ a lovely break in Europe," he said to Lily. "I (8.) _____ some cousins in London who (9.) _____ a large house. They (10.) _____ a surprise when I phone them up."

Leo, Lily's husband, stopped the car in front of the door to the Governor's villa. The two agents climbed out. They were dressed in smart black suits which they had put on in Lily's bathroom. Leo nodded and drove on. The two men waved goodbye. The wide driveway was brightly lit. Flower tubs stood on both sides of the road which led from the gate in the garden wall up to the entrance of the villa. One after the other, limousines drove through the gate and then stopped in front of the steps into the building. Men in smart suits helped the women out of the cars. The women were wearing evening dresses and high-heeled shoes. There was cheerful laughter as the men replaced fallen scarves around the women's pale shoulders. Nimble fingers checked elaborate hairstyles, making sure that every single hair and hairpin was still in its place.

Übung 84: Unterstreichen Sie die Synonyme folgender Wörter!
(1. roadway 2. pair 3. just 4. to forward 5. to fetch 6. subordinate 7. position 8. present 9. pleasant)

Hunter and Percy walked up the drive. They followed behind a couple who had arrived shortly before them. At the door, Hunter gave the invitations to the security guard.
Percy had asked the Headquarters in London to send the invitations and had collected them that morning from the British Embassy in the town. The agents were named as junior diplomats in the British Corps: Hunter as the top candidate who would take over the role of the current Ambassador on the island in the next few years and Percy as his right-hand man. The security guard wished them an enjoyable evening and let them in.

The walls and the floor of the entrance hall were marble. A glittering chandelier shone down from the ceiling. Excited chatter surrounded them as they walked into the middle of the room. To the left, double doors opened into a room where there was a bar and long tables bearing plates of food. Guests were milling around with plates and cups. It seemed as though the buffet had already been open for some time. A waiter approached bearing a tray. Hunter took a glass of champagne. Percy took one too. Their glasses clinked as they toasted each other.

Then Hunter and Percy separated. The plan for the evening was to make contacts.

Übung 85: Verwandeln Sie die Sätze ins Past Perfect!
Beispiel: We are going home.   We had gone home.

1. Percy is speaking with Mogudi.

_____

2. The guests are eating canapés.

_____

3. The security men are checking the invitations.

_____

4. The host is greeting the new arrivals.

_____

5. The woman are taking off their hats and scarves.

_____

6. The men are straightening their ties.

_____

Hunter scanned the rooms for the Governor. He wanted to grill him. To do that, he had to speak to him alone. Unfortunately, Mogudi was deep in conversation with three broad-shouldered men in designer dinner jackets. The conversation seemed to be taking a long time. The agent leaned casually on the frame of one of the high windows which looked out onto the garden. He watched the other guests who were standing in twos or small groups. Many were laughing; others were talking animatedly.

A woman in a flowing silk dress suddenly appeared at Hunter's side. She pushed her champagne glass towards his and looked at him directly in the eye. She spoke to him in English. He recognised a slight Russian accent. When he asked her about it, she said, "Well guessed! So you *are* the right man for international relations!"

At first, Hunter did not understand what she meant. However, as she continued talking, it was evident that she thought he was the next British Ambassador, as it had said on the invitation.

"I've been finding out about you," she said. "You'll be having a say in the matter soon too."

She placed her hand on his arm. Gently but firmly, she pulled him towards the French windows. Before Hunter followed the Russian woman outside, he glanced over his shoulder. Percy was approaching Mogudi. That was not what they had agreed. Hunter sighed and thought, "Just don't do anything silly, lad."

The moon shone down from the night sky onto the gardens. There were torches at the edge of the gravel path. In the flickering light, couples were walking through the extensive grounds. The woman stopped. She kept hold of Hunter's arm and turned to look at him.

Übung 86: Wie lautet die Nationalität zu folgenden Ländern?

1. Russia   _____

2. Holland   _____

3. Switzerland　　　　　_____

4. Cuba　　　　　　　_____

5. Peru　　　　　　　_____

6. Spain　　　　　　　_____

7. Scotland　　　　　　_____

"My name is Natascha," she began. "My bosses are in Moscow. We've recently resumed our business relationship with Mogudi. Unfortunately, he's not as co-operative as he was when he started his job. Your Ambassador is still as neutral as ever. But you're young, a man of the world! You don't look like a decrepit old Englishman. You're brave, aren't you?"

Hunter confirmed what she said with a confident smile. "Of course I'm brave! Why, do you need a hero?"

She heard the flirtatious tone in his voice and suddenly began speaking in a very business-like manner. "You bet! The situation here on the island is ideal. Hardly any tourists, it's cut off from the major oceanic trading routes, the harbour is small but it's in good shape. The only people who are in our way are the Argentinians. I don't know whether you know about the incident this morning …."

The agent nodded. Natascha kept talking. It seemed as though her Russian bosses were working in a similar line of business to the Argentinians. From the small clues she gave, Hunter deduced that the two countries were in each other's way. On several occasions, she called the South Americans 'fools' who would ruin everything with their unprofessional attitude. Hunter wondered what the woman actually wanted from him.

Übung 87: Unterstreichen Sie alle Pronomen!

"Of course, the English aren't interested in these matters. At least, that's what your Ambassador here is saying. But you might be interested one day, when your Ambassador goes?" She looked meaningfully at him. He waited.

"In other words ... This is the deal: you help us to get rid of the Argentinians. You won't have to worry about anything if you work with us. It may even be very profitable for you. As long as no one knows about what's going on because stupid idiots are aiming their nuclear weapons at fishermen and sinking their own ships in the harbour."

The agent pretended to be interested in her suggestion. "What do you think we should do?"

"Put pressure on Mogudi. He should drive the Argentinians out of the contract. After all, we're paying him good money to test here. And if you were involved as a business partner, you could say to him that England, like Russia, doesn't particularly like it when his natives wave their banners about in the market square. He's getting money to give his people here a good life. But it hasn't been good here for a while."

Übung 88: Lesen Sie weiter und beantworten Sie die Fragen!

1. How does Natascha let Hunter know that she will come back?

_____

2. What does Hunter then do?

_____

107

3. Who starts talking to Hunter?

_____

4. Which words describe the British Ambassador's suit?

_____

5. Did the Ambassador know a long time in advance that Hunter would be at the Reception?

_____

She grabbed the empty champagne glasses and hurried back into the room. With a wink, she indicated to Hunter that she would return immediately. He did not wait, but followed her. From the French windows, he could see that Percy was still talking to Mogudi.

The British Ambassador came up to Hunter. He was an old man and wore an elegant suit which looked rather old-fashioned. The Diplomat had learned only that day that his potential successor would be at the Reception. He congratulated Hunter and asked him about his career. The Ambassador had met Percy that day in the Embassy when he was collecting the invitations sent from London. He thought Percy was a dashing and worthy assistant for a man like Hunter.

Hunter was not enjoying the conversation. He remembered Walter saying that the Americans did not trust their own Ambassadors. That seemed to be the case here too. The Secret Service had not considered it necessary to inform the old man that agents had infiltrated the island.

The Ambassador was giving Hunter an invitation. He said that if the agent wanted to visit him in his office or privately, he would be very happy to give him some tips.

Übung 89: Setzen Sie die Adjektive in der jeweils richtigen Reihenfolge ein!

A (1. short/fat) _____ _____ man with (2. grey/curly) _____

_____ hair and a (3. handsome/large) _____

face is travelling to a (4. tropical/remote/small) _____

_____ _____ island. He is wearing a

(5. striped/new/red) _____ _____ _____ T-shirt and is

carrying a (6. leather/worn) _____ _____ suitcase. Inside

the suitcase there is an (7. expensive/new) _____

_____ camera and some (8. second-hand/cheap) _____

_____ books.

As Hunter looked over to Mogudi, he saw that he was talking to a tall man with long black hair. Percy had disappeared. At least, Hunter could not see him anywhere in the crowd of other guests.

The Russian woman returned with two full glasses. Hunter excused himself, saying that he had to look for his fellow Diplomat. In truth, he needed a moment to get his thoughts together.

He made his way to the toilets. A stocky man stood next to him at the washbasins. The man started speaking. It was not long before he referred to Hunter as the next British representative on the island. The agent was surprised at how quickly his alias had become known and how credible it seemed to be. The British Secret Service had done good work. His colleagues had presumably given the relevant international secret services a CV which coordinated exactly with his role here.

ÜBUNG 90

*Übung 90: Setzen Sie die richtige Zeitform von **to work** ein!*

1. I _____ every day.
2. I _____ just _____ .
3. I _____ yesterday.
4. I _____ _____ now.
5. I _____ _____ _____ for one hour.
6. I _____ already _____ that morning.
7. I _____ _____ _____ tomorrow.
8. I _____ _____ tomorrow.
9. I _____ not _____ _____ _____ any longer!
10. I _____ _____ _____ _____ longer, but I've changed my mind.

The man with the black moustache had obviously been drinking. He hiccupped loudly and talked in a familiar tone to Hunter. There was a pregnant pause in his flow of conversation as he mentioned his surname. Hunter immediately recognised the link to the leading Italian Mafia syndicate. The man saw that Hunter had made the connection.

"Let me say this between us. Your old Ambassador looks good in his tails, but what we need here is fresh blood! The Argentinians aren't much use any more. The Russians want everything for themselves. What do you think? Mogudi agrees. No more tests, just a few goods smuggled through. A bit of money laundered here, a few crates of dynamite there. The location of the islands is ideal." Hunter had heard it all before.

Übung 91: Setzen Sie die Verben in der richtigen Zeitform ein!

All at once, the noise in the room (1. become) _____ louder. The music was drowned out by voices. The men (2. look) _____ curiously at each other. They (3. leave) _____ the toilets together. Something seemed to have got massively out of hand. Security guards (4. run) _____ down the wide marble staircase; women (5. scream) _____; shots (6. fire) _____. Hunter (7. push) _____ his way through the crowd of people. He wanted to get to the centre of the riot to see what (8. happen) _____.

There was a fight going on in the middle of the room. The Russian woman stood facing the man with the long hair who had previously been speaking with the Governor. They were threatening each other and held their guns drawn. Mogudi had disappeared. Hunter looked around for Percy, but he had been swallowed up too. The short Italian man appeared next to him. "Oh please, you idiots! Both of you! And at a party as well!"

The security guards surrounded the guests. The guests formed a circle around the Russian woman and the tall man, who was most certainly Argentinian. Both stood stock-still.

A plump man stepped forward out of the crowd and moved between them to calm the situation. He spoke with a Russian accent. In a casual tone, he muttered something about a lovers' tiff. He grabbed the man and the woman by the hand as if they were children. He took both their guns away and led them to a side room.

The party continued. It seemed as though events like this were normal in these circles. Hunter was amazed.

Übung 92: Unterstreichen Sie das „schwarze Schaf"!

1. chamber, room, hall, auditorium, door
2. head, throat, temples, ache, forehead, neck
3. silently, noiselessly, nervously, wordlessly, soundlessly
4. stupid, intelligent, slow-witted, simple, foolish
5. jacket, anorak, socks, coat, blazer, mackintosh

He crept after the three people. The door of the side room had not even closed when there came the dull thud of a bullet fired through a silencer. Through the gap in the door, Hunter saw that the Russian man had shot the Argentinian at point-blank range in the temples. Natascha was standing silently nearby. The murderer slapped her hard on her head and hissed something to her in Russian. Hunter did not understand everything. However, the woman's stupid behaviour had presumably made the man angry.

A telephone rang. Angrily, the Russian pulled his mobile phone out of his jacket pocket. He yelled a greeting. His face darkened. When the conversation had ended, he turned off the phone. He ordered the girl to hurry up. "Get a move on, Natascha! Go and get on with your job! Mogudi has disappeared!"

Horrified, she said, "But Marek was allocated to him today! It was those damned Argentinians! Or perhaps the little Mafia guy!"

He interrupted her brusquely. "I don't care who it was, just get Mogudi back. We need him. He knows far too much. We'll never find a puppet Governor like him again. *And* his lousy people are still voting for him!"

Natascha did not move. The Russian slapped her face again. "Get a move on, Natascha! It's your neck on the block as well! The people in Moscow will kill us!"

Übung 93: Übersetzen Sie!

1. Um den Leuten zu helfen, könnten wir ihnen Geld geben.

2. Um das Problem zu lösen, müssten wir viele Maßnahmen einleiten.

3. Um zu einer Verbesserung beizutragen, müssten die Leute viel ausgeben.

4. Um ihm zum Sieg zu verhelfen, sollten wir ihm zujubeln.

5. Um den Frieden zu sichern, müssten wir unsere Waffen niederlegen.

Quickly, Hunter moved away from the door and into the crowd. He watched as Natascha came out of the room and hurried through the guests to the door. She held her watch close to her mouth. The agent presumed that it had an integrated radio. Keeping his distance, he followed her. He had not yet reached the exit when Percy intercepted him in front of the door. The young man paid no attention to Hunter's questions and pulled him outside behind him. Hunter had lost sight of Natascha. He stumbled after his assistant, who had his hand clasped tightly around his wrist. Hunter wanted to free himself, but Percy's long, thin fingers were too strong.

They hurried down the drive, went through the gate and then turned left. They ran about a hundred metres down the road. Hunter panted. Percy was striding ahead with his long legs. Hunter had to make almost twice as many steps to keep up with him. They reached the car in which Leo was sitting at the steering wheel. Percy threw open the front door and pushed Hunter into the passenger seat. The younger man climbed into the back seat. Even before he had shut the rear door, he shouted to their driver, "Step on it, Leo!"

The tyres squealed. Leo moved quickly into top gear and the car flew down the road. The Governor's villa was on the outskirts of the town. Leo kept driving. He ignored a red light. Unconcerned, he maintained his speed. The road slowly became narrower. The houses and gardens petered out and they left the built-up area.

When they came to the crossroads, Leo turned right and drove up towards the cliffs. The car's headlights shone onto the edge of the road. It fell steeply into the sea.

> *Übung 94: Finden Sie passende Synonyme für die Adverbien!*

Hunter turned around to his colleague. He wanted to ask something but then (1. abruptly) _____ noticed that there was another person on the back seat next to Percy. The man was broad and was sitting hunched up (2. unhappily) _____. His seatbelt ran (3. obliquely) _____ across his chest, crushing his fashionably large dinner jacket, which hung (4. strangely) _____ on his fat body. In the darkness, Hunter could not see the man's eyes behind his thick glasses, but (5. supposedly) _____ they were directed towards the floor of the car. At least, that was what Hunter concluded from the way the other man held his head.

"This is Mr Mogudi," explained Percy. The man raised his head (6. momentarily) _____ when he recognised his name. He did not say anything and then lowered his head again. "What?" cried Hunter. "We had a little chat at the party," explained Percy (7. casually) _____. "The Italians, the Argentinians and the Russians were all interested in him, so I thought I'd do my bit for England."

These brief explanations did not seem sufficient for the Governor. With a thin voice, he said from the back seat, "Thank you, gentlemen. You have saved my life."

Hunter still did not understand what was going on. He waited until the man spoke again. His story was relatively short. The agent already knew most of it from the stories which Lily and Leo had told. Mogudi described in detail how he had tried to encourage investors to bring foreign currency into his small country two years previously. There was hardly any business on the islands and very little industry. He believed that tourism was the only option that his people had to survive international competition.

Übung 95: Bilden Sie sinnvolle Wörter aus dem Buchstabenchaos!

However, the people who expressed some (1. tientser) _____ in his ideas had other things in mind. They came from South (2. aiAmcer) _____ and Russia and were not interested in helping the small island (3. tpionpoula) _____. Instead of hotels, they wanted stores for (4. aimomnunit) _____, and instead of sandy beaches, they wanted sand banks for testing (5. anerucl) _____ weapons. The first (6. naectcid) _____ occurred only a few months after Mogudi had taken up his post. On one of the (7. nidssla) _____, the inhabitants were exposed to so much (8. irtandioa) _____ that it was impossible for him and his Ministers to keep the matter quiet. After that, the Russians and the Argentinians had withdrawn. The country fell further into decline and the people grew poorer and poorer.

At this point in the story, Leo let out a loud "I see!" The plump man with the glasses was unperturbed. He continued his report.

The Americans had contacted him a few months previously. They had similar plans to the Argentinians and Russians and had offered him money. The Governor agreed. In order to rehabilitate his country, he emphasised. But then the South Americans and the Russians had come back onto the scene. He gave them the right to conduct their illegal weapons testing too.

For some months, the world had been unaware of what was happening. The situation had only got out of control when there was another accident during a weapons test. Two of the islands were evacuated, but it was too late. Once again, deformed children were born and people died. Unfortunately, Mogudi regretted, his men had not been quick enough in removing the evidence.

Hunter thought back to the children in the Foreign Aid Centre. He shuddered with horror at the man on the back seat.

Übung 96: Unterstreichen Sie die indirekte Rede!

Mogudi was defending his position. He said that everything he had done had been for the benefit of his country, even the fact that he had now given the Italians the opportunity to conduct weapons transactions and to launder money in his country.

Leo rounded a bend on the narrow road. Percy was thrown against the Governor.

"Watch out!" the man shouted indignantly. Then, in a more friendly tone, he added, "You must excuse me, my nerves are shattered. My people are totally right. The tests must end. It is better to wait a hundred years for holidaymakers than to kill our own descendants and leave the islands uninhabitable for ever. Please, help us."

Hunter did not know what to think about Mogudi. Undoubtedly, the justifications which he gave were watertight. However, there was something about what he said or, more precisely, in the way in which he said it, that made Hunter suspicious.

"Where are we actually going?" the agent asked Leo.

"To my cousin's. We'll be safe there for the time being. She lives with her family on a tiny farm on the other side of the island."

Percy interrupted the driver. He glanced behind him through the rear windscreen and said, "Looks like we're not the only visitors."

Hunter checked in the wing mirror. Indeed, lights had appeared on the road and seemed to be drawing nearer. Leo pressed his foot down on the accelerator. The car was making a loud noise. Hunter was worried. What would happen if it broke down?

Übung 97: Setzen Sie die richtigen Relativpronomen ein!

1. People _____ drive fast are dangerous on the roads.

2. A driver _____ car breaks down should telephone the rescue service.

3. The men _____ are following us seem to be in a hurry.

4. The headlights _____ he had turned on were very bright.

5. The people from _____ we borrowed the car will be angry.

6. It was a road _____ barely anyone used.

The lights were coming closer. Now and again, they disappeared briefly when there was a bend in the coast road. However, there was no doubt that the pursuers were hot on their trail.

"There are two cars, aren't there?" asked Hunter.

"At least two," said Percy. Because of all the bends in the narrow road, it was hard to say exactly how many headlights there were behind them.

Mogudi was silent. He pulled at his seatbelt. There was obviously something on his mind. He cleared his throat several times, but said nothing. Instead, he kept looking across to Percy. The Governor's glances irritated the junior agent. Percy looked back at the man next to him and then turned around to check the road behind them.

Now there were barely fifty metres between them and the bumper of the first pursuer. The men in Leo's car were now certain that there were at least three cars following them. Shots fired out behind them. Hunter wound down the car window. He released the safety catch on his pistol. Stupidly, Percy had only brought two small guns with him in his sports bag. They hardly had any ammunition and would have to economise. Hunter hesitated. He did not want to use up all his bullets. To do so would certainly be a fatal error given the crowd of pursuers behind them. All the same, he was ready to shoot.

On the back seat, Percy copied him. He wound down the window and was ready for action. He whispered to Mogudi, "Don't worry, you're quite safe."

The Governor sank deeper into the seat and remained silent.

Übung 98: Formen Sie die Sätze wie im Beispiel um!
Beispiel: Mogudi said nothing. Mogudi did not say anything.

1. Hunter saw nobody.

_____

2. There was nothing in the boot of the car.

_____

3. He had no bullets left.

4. The Governor trusted no one.

5. The car never broke down.

6. There was no rust on the bodywork.

7. He missed none of his targets.

"Wow!" shouted Percy. A bullet tore through the rear windscreen and buried itself in the driver's headrest. Leo swore loudly. Mogudi said nothing. The bullet had flown through the windscreen directly over his head. He shrank deeper into the seat.

"Down!" yelled Hunter. Percy obeyed the command and squashed himself onto the floor of the car. It was a mystery to Hunter how the tall man had managed to make himself so small between the back seat and the front seat. But there was no time now to solve the mystery. Another bullet tore through the wing mirror.

Leo muttered, "I've had enough! I haven't even had the car for one day!"

He steered the car left. There was a small hill at the side of the road. The tyres rumbled over grass and gravel. The headlights of the first pursuer came up behind them. Then, the pursuers drove their car up alongside Leo's. The two cars raced along the road.

Percy fired his gun through the window. He saw how the man on the back seat of the other car crumpled. The man beside him shouted. He shot at Percy, who ducked very quickly. The shot simply hit the metal of the car door. Hunter fired a direct shot at the driver of the other car: it was the Russian who he had been in the side room with Natascha. The agent's shot only grazed the man. Leo continued driving half on the road and half on the grass. The car shook violently.

Übung 99: Markieren Sie mit richtig ✔ oder falsch –!

1. Leo is angry because he has not had the car for very long.
2. The ground at the side of the road is flat.
3. The car behind Leo's does not have its headlights switched on.
4. The two cars drive along side by side.
5. Both Percy and Hunter fire a shot.
6. Percy's shot is less successful that Hunter's.
7. Natascha is in the car behind Leo's.

"Hold on tight!" Leo shouted. He steered unexpectedly towards the right. His car banged against the other vehicle. As quick as lightening, Hunter withdrew his arm back into the car. Leo took another swing and rammed against his opponent. The Russian driver lost control. He held onto the steering wheel with both hands. The weapon which he had been aiming at Hunter fell into his lap. Leo was merciless. He rammed the other car again. The car swerved to the right and moved off the road. The brakes squealed. Then the car fell like an arrow over the cliff. There was a crashing noise as it fell down the cliffs. A beam of light briefly lit up the night sky as the car burst into flames.

Leo cheered. However, there was no time for celebration as there was another car rapidly approaching from behind. He braked hard. Leo's passengers saw the other car drive past them. Leo changed into reverse gear and turned. He pushed hard on the accelerator. His car raced down the road in the opposite direction from which it had come.

Übung 100: Setzen Sie das richtige Wort ein!

1. To cheer _____ a friend.
2. To think _____ a problem.
3. To fill _____ the gaps.
4. To bring _____ children.
5. To put _____ a suggestion.
6. To make _____ an answer.

Leo's action had irritated the occupants of the third vehicle. As Leo drove towards them, instead of racing away from him, they slowed down. Leo maintained his speed. In the meantime, the second car had turned around in the narrow road and was accelerating towards them. Hunter's car was now in the middle. He prayed that Leo knew what he was doing. Leo was grinning madly and gripped the steering wheel tightly.

Just before they collided with the third car, Hunter grabbed the steering wheel. Leo's car turned with its boot towards the hill. Clods of earth skidded beneath the tyres. The wheels spun. The occupants were thrown first backwards and then forwards. Hunter's head hit the car door. Behind him, he felt Percy being thrown violently against his seat.

The people in the second car behind Leo realised too late that the other vehicle was coming towards them. They collided head-on and remained wedged together on the road. Leo accelerated down the hill. He hit both cars and slowly pushed them towards the cliffs. Then, all of a sudden, he lost control.

"Everyone out!" he yelled. Mogudi pulled frantically at his seatbelt. Percy released him. The four men jumped out of the car. The three cars hurtled towards the precipice. There were shouts from the other cars. Doors slammed. The vehicles fell over the edge and clattered noisily down the cliff face. There was an explosion, the sound of shattering glass and loud crashing noises. Once again, the sky lit up for second. Then the men heard the cars fall into the water far below.

Übung 101: Bilden Sie Wortfamilien aus den beiden Adjektiven!
(late, bad)

1. der Komparativ: _____

2. der Superlativ: _____

3. das Adverb: _____

4. das Substantiv: _____

1. der Komparativ: _____

2. der Superlativ: _____

3. das Adverb: _____

4. das Substantiv: _____

Then there was silence on the coast road. Hunter raised himself up off the ground. He was aching all over. Percy lay crumpled on the tarmac beside him. The agent wanted to check that his colleague was OK, but Percy got up, swearing loudly. Leo walked towards them. "Everything alright?" he enquired.

"You drive like a maniac!" praised Hunter. Percy wanted to agree but there was someone approaching them. Natascha stood with her gun raised in front of Mogudi, who was kneeling on the road. Her dress was totally ruined. There were shreds of material everywhere. Her hair was standing wildly on her head. She had a wound on her forehead. She must have hit her head during the collision. She was laughing hysterically as she pressed the barrel of the gun to the Governor's neck.

Somebody else had survived the crash. It was the short fat Italian man. He was dragging his leg behind him as he approached the group. His submachine gun looked like a giant's toy in the hands of a dwarf.

"He's mine!" he shouted to Natascha. He pointed at Mogudi. Mogudi was moaning to himself. Natascha laughed insanely.

The Mafia man thundered, "Move away! I said, 'he's mine!'"

"Natascha!" interrupted Hunter.

"I'm over here!" she cried. She removed her gun from Mogudi's neck and shot in Hunter's direction. She missed him by a hair's breadth. She laughed. Then, suddenly, she went silent. She choked. Her eyes lost their mad stare. Her gun fell from her hand to the ground. Quickly, Mogudi grabbed the pistol and got up. Natascha pressed her palms to her neck. She stared at Percy. He had wanted to protect Hunter. In defence, he had fired a shot. He watched silently as the Russian woman fell to the ground. Blood streamed through her fingers from the wound in her neck. He must have hit an artery. With his gun lowered, Percy stood still and watched. He had never killed anyone before.

Übung 102: Übersetzen Sie!

1. Ich habe es machen müssen.

___

2. Wir sollten ihn unterrichten.

___

3. Sie hat es sehen können.

___

4. Sie haben es uns sagen wollen.

___

5. Ich hätte es machen müssen.

___

6. Wir hätten ihn lehren sollen.

___

7. Sie hatte es sehen können.

___

8. Sie hatten es uns sagen wollen.

___

"Thank you, young man," croaked Mogudi. He aimed Natascha's gun at Percy. "And don't you do that to me again!" he bellowed at the Italian.
"It was only a joke, boss," the man retorted.

"I don't understand …" said Percy. Mogudi's laugh cut him short. The Governor, who, a short time before, had been sitting pitifully on the back seat, was now anything but frightened. He walked towards the young agent, grabbed the gun out of his hand and calmly placed the pistol to Percy's forehead.

"You keep out of it!" he warned Hunter, who wanted to intervene. The Governor shouted at the agents. "Put your weapons down!" he yelled.

Hunter did as he was told. However, he threw his pistol behind him. "You idiot! I meant, give them to me!" snarled Mogudi. Hunter was silent.

The Italian man walked towards Hunter with ropes to tie the agent's hands behind his back. Hunter wanted to punch him, but when he saw Percy with the gun to his head, he decided not to. The Mafia man tightened the ropes. Mogudi was watching. "Thank you, men, for getting those unbearable Russians and Argentinians off my back. I would much prefer to co-operate with the Italians."

The fat man with the moustache had finished tying up Hunter. "That's a good bit of work! What shall I do with him now?" He pointed at Hunter. "Throw him into the sea?" asked the Italian. Mogudi sniggered.

"Don't swim out too far!" warned the Mafia man. "We wouldn't want you to find any nuclear bombs, would we?"

Mogudi's stopped sniggering. "What?" he shouted.

"Nuclear bombs. Or perhaps you think we Italians are testing our weapons in our own country when everything's so well prepared here?"

Mogudi was shocked. "But I thought we were just laundering a bit of money and smuggling through a few weapons for you?"

"Oh yes," confirmed the Italian. "But we'll also want to test the weapons that we're moving through your country."

Übung 103: Welcher Satz enthält die richtige Zeitform?

1. Ich kann dich nicht weinen sehen.
   a) ☐ I cannot watch you crying.
   b) ☐ I could not watch you crying.
   c) ☐ I could not have watched you crying.

2. Er musste nach dem Unfall wieder laufen lernen.
   a) ☐ He will have to learn to walk again after the accident.
   b) ☐ He had to learn to walk again after the accident.
   c) ☐ He has to learn to walk again after the accident.

3. Ich hätte es ihnen geben können.
   a) ☐ I could have given it to you.
   b) ☐ I can give it to you.
   c) ☐ I will be able to give it to you.

4. Der Staatschef wollte den Agenten sprechen.
   a) ☐ The Governor had wanted to speak to the agent.
   b) ☐ The Governor had wanted to speak to the agent.
   c) ☐ The Governor wanted to speak to the agent.

In the confusion, Percy seized his opportunity. He used his elbow to ram the Governor in the ribs. The Governor, caught off guard by the attack, staggered. Percy kicked him. Mogudi stumbled to his knees. The young agent gave him a blow to his neck. He fell forwards. Percy grabbed the weapon which Mogudi had dropped.
"You keep out of it!" yelled the Mafia man at Percy. "Or your mate here will get it in the head!" To confirm up his words, he brandished his submachine gun in the air and let off a volley of shots towards the sky.

Then there was the sound of another shot, but this time only one. Leo was standing at the side of the road with Hunter's gun. He had shot the Italian directly in the chest. Blood spewed from the injured man. Barely two seconds later, he was dead.

"Leo!" exclaimed Hunter. "You're fantastic!" Percy hurried to his boss and untied the ropes. Then he re-used them to tie up Mogudi, who was still lying unconscious on the ground. "Finished!" said Percy as he stood up.
Hunter jumped to his younger colleague's side. Gratefully, he slapped him on the back. As a joke, Percy prodded his boss lightly in his ribs. "Damn!" cried Hunter.
"Sorry!" stuttered Percy. "Did I hurt you?" The junior agent stopped. He looked up. Leo walked towards them. His mouth fell open.
With trembling fingers, Hunter fished the cartridge with its dangerous content matter out of his jacket pocket. The container was damp. There were droplets of liquid on the outside of it. The men looked at each other. From the ground, Mogudi moaned loudly.
Carefully, Hunter took a handkerchief from his other pocket. His hands were still trembling as he wiped the cartridge. The droplets disappeared and Hunter saw that the cartridge was undamaged. "It was condensation!" he said with relief. He wrapped the cartridge carefully in the handkerchief.
"Let's go," he said.

Übung 104: Setzen Sie die richtigen Zeitformen der Verben ein!

Lily (1. serve) _____ island specialities for dinner. They all (2. sit) _____ around the table in her house and (3. tell) _____ her about the chase. Hunter smiled when he (4. see) _____ how proud Lily (5. be) _____ of her husband. She (6. hang) _____ onto his every word. She was genuinely enthusiastic as she (7. listen) _____ to his story. During the thrilling parts, she covered her face with her hands. Leo liked entertaining his wife. They (8. be) _____ a lovely couple.

Percy and Hunter had already been thanked by Captain Martens and their boss Mrs Callaghan over the telephone. Mogudi was now in prison at the British Embassy and would appear before an international court in the following few weeks. Nevertheless, because there were no other witnesses apart from him, it was doubtful whether anyone else would be convicted. The Argentinians had already said that they would make enquiries concerning the corrupt individuals in the navy who had misused warships for such horrifying and illegal operations without the knowledge of the Argentinian Government.

Übung 105: Unterstreichen Sie die Hauptsätze!

1. Because Leo had had so much excitement, he was very tired.
2. As it was late, the children had to go to bed.
3. The men chatted while the women organised the children.
4. Since there was only one witness, there was little evidence.
5. There were many issues to solve and the work would take several months.

129

The contents of the cartridge had been examined by the Secret Service laboratory in London. The cartridge *had* contained highly radioactive matter. The torpedoes fitted with the cartridges were extremely dangerous. An English weapons inspection team was helping the Argentinian Navy to salvage the wreck in the island's harbour. Too much had happened. Everyone wanted to be certain that the islanders would not be subjected to further danger, for instance from the unscrupulous use of weapons which were supposed to be part of a disarmament exercise. At least, that was what the Argentinian Government said.

Übung 106: Enträtseln Sie das Lösungswort!

1. Object of a shot
2. Large explosive weapon
3. South American country
4. Small hand gun
5. Sunken ship
6. Dangerous
7. Release of energy
8. Missile from a gun
9. Opposite of failure

Lösung: _ _ _ _ _ _ _ _ _

The Russian Government also distanced itself from the events. Russian politicians claimed that certain individuals were responsible. The Government's explanations were confusing. Natascha and her accomplices were said to work in underworld circles, which meant that they were traitors to the Russian Secret Service.

At least there was no danger of any more nuclear weapons testing in the years to come. The United Nations declared the group of islands a special protectorate. They wanted to keep a close eye on everything that happened on the islands and all the political decisions in the future.

"Why don't you put yourself forward as the next Governor of the islands?" Percy asked Leo. Before her husband could reply, Lily said, "Forget it! I think we've all had quite enough adventures already!" Leo grinned.

Übung 107: Welche Phrase hat welche Bedeutung?

1. The Union Jack
2. Hobson's choice
3. A cheap Jack
4. An Aladdin's cave
5. A jack of all trades
6. An Achilles' heel
7. A jack-in-the-box
8. The Jolly Roger
9. Jackpot

a) ☐ The pirate flag
b) ☐ A room filled with treasures
c) ☐ Somebody with a lot of skills
d) ☐ A children's toy
e) ☐ A fatal weakness
f) ☐ The flag of the United Kingdom
g) ☐ A large amount of money
h) ☐ A mean, dishonest person
i) ☐ No choice

Before the children were sent to bed, Hunter said he had a surprise for the family. They all followed him outside. Lily squealed with delight and Leo cheered. The children laughed and shouted at one another. Their grandmother hung onto the arm of her second daughter and said, "That's amazing!"

Übung 108: Setzen Sie die fehlenden Wörter in die jeweils richtigen Lücken ein!
(loudly, door, list, explained, courageous, expenses)

Standing in front of the (1.) _____ was a brand-new minibus. It was painted in the colours of the Union Jack. Hunter (2.) _____ that the Secret Service had wanted to thank Leo for his (3.) _____ support.

In fact, Mrs Callaghan had complained so (4.) _____ to Hunter when she saw his provisional list of (5.) _____ for his assignment that Hunter had added something else to the (6.) _____.

He had bought Leo the most expensive and most practical vehicle for a large family that he could find on the island. He paid extra to have it painted red, white and blue. Surprised by his own boldness, he added the minibus to the expenses list for Mrs Callaghan.

"Shall we go out for a quick spin?" offered Leo grinning. "Perhaps out to the cliffs?"

Abschlusstest

Übung 1: Welche Wörter gehören zu welchen Wortarten?

1. Government, ship, island, Pacific, taxi
2. angrily, abroad, harshly, today, suddenly
3. shoot, test, discover, demonstrate, drive
4. hot, exhausted, Russian, deformed, curly
5. or, but, and, since, unless, because
6. him, she, we, our, you, them
7. under, up, across, through, down
8. Ouch!, Oh!, Gosh!, Yuck!

a) ☐ Verbs
b) ☐ Interjections
c) ☐ Conjunctions
d) ☐ Prepositions
e) ☐ Nouns
f) ☐ Adverbs
g) ☐ Pronouns
h) ☐ Adjectives

Übung 2: Setzen Sie das richtige Pronomen ein!

Lily invited Hunter into her house and introduced (1.) _____ to her family. "My grandmother lives with (2.) _____," (3.) _____ said. "(4.) _____ all live together. (5.) _____ have one sister and one brother. My sister is called Rita and (6.) _____ has two daughters. My brother's name is Richard. (7.) _____ is a student. Leo is my husband and (8.) _____ are all very happy living here."

Übung 3: Setzen Sie die richtigen Konjunktionen ein!

1. Leo was tired _____ happy.

2. The children were aged eleven _____ eight.

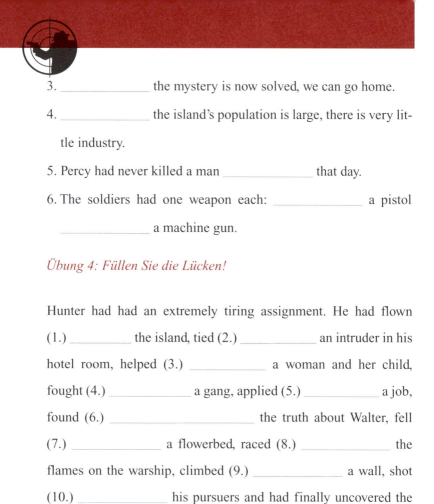

3. _____ the mystery is now solved, we can go home.

4. _____ the island's population is large, there is very little industry.

5. Percy had never killed a man _____ that day.

6. The soldiers had one weapon each: _____ a pistol _____ a machine gun.

Übung 4: Füllen Sie die Lücken!

Hunter had had an extremely tiring assignment. He had flown (1.) _____ the island, tied (2.) _____ an intruder in his hotel room, helped (3.) _____ a woman and her child, fought (4.) _____ a gang, applied (5.) _____ a job, found (6.) _____ the truth about Walter, fell (7.) _____ a flowerbed, raced (8.) _____ the flames on the warship, climbed (9.) _____ a wall, shot (10.) _____ his pursuers and had finally uncovered the facts. Now all he wanted to do was go home!

Übung 5: Ordnen Sie die Adjektive zu einem sinnvollen Wort!

1. The aeroplane ticket was very (esxipveen) _____.

2. Hunter knew very well that his assignment would be extremely (udilftfic) _____.

3. Percy was an (einsttahiucs) _____ colleague.

4. Lily's grandmother was warm and (lfdyrien) _____.

5. There were (frliicnkge) _____ torches along the path.

Übung 6: Finden Sie die Substantive!

1. Jamaica, Rügen, Greenland and Australia are all _____.

2. Pistols, machine guns, rifles and torpedoes are all _____.

3. Aeroplanes, taxis, ships, bicycles and cars are all types of _____.

4. Suitcases, shoulder bags, wallets and handbags are all pieces of _____.

5. Bananas, pineapples, oranges and mangoes are all tropical _____.

6. Russian, Dutch, Argentinian and British are all _____.

7. The wrist, the neck, the forehead and the stomach are all part of the _____.

Übung 7: Unterstreichen Sie das „schwarze Schaf!"

1. sudden, abrupt, rapid, quick, slow
2. blue, yellow, bright, red, black, green
3. fatigued, energetic, weary, tired, worn out
4. happy, pleased, delighted, glad, discontented
5. poor, rich, wealthy, affluent, prosperous

Übung 8: Setzen Sie die fehlenden Satzzeichen ein!

Where are you going asked the lorry driver
I m going back to my hotel said Hunter
At 10 00 p m they arrived at the hotel
Gosh exclaimed the driver   Is that where you re staying
Hunter replied that the hotel had been allocated by the Secret Service

Übung 9: Schreiben Sie die Sätze aus!

1. There's no one there!

___

2. We haven't been to the beach!

___

3. They couldn't have seen the explosion.

___

4. You're going to find out soon!

___

5. I've wanted to visit that island!

___

Übung 10: Finden Sie die Adjektive zu den Substantiven!

1. sadness   _____

2. anger   _____

3. relevance   _____

4. health   _____

5. heat   _____

6. warmth   _____

7. ability   _____

8. power   _____

Übung 11: Wie lauten die Infinitive der Verben?

1. spoke   _____
2. shook   _____
3. fell   _____
4. sank   _____
5. said   _____
6. began   _____
7. held   _____
8. paid   _____
9. told   _____
10. got   _____
11. became   _____
12. found   _____
13. thought   _____

Lösungen

Übung 1: Captain, radio, smile, face, monitor, torpedo, progress, water, gaze, window, buoy, target, torpedo, metres, waves, afternoon, buoy, Binoculars

Übung 2: 1.The ship sails into the harbour. 2. The captain is angry. 3. The soldier gives him the binoculars. 4. The man wears a dark-blue cap. 5. The captain wants to detonate the torpedo. 6. The sailors see the buoy in the distance.

Übung 3: 1. to fall 2. to say 3. to speak 4. to begin 5. to sink 6. to shake 7. to pay 8. to tell 9. to get 10. to hold

Übung 4: 1. The soldier 2. To thank the man 3. Dark-blue 4. Twist his hat in his hands 5. Very strong.

Übung 5: 1. an 2. a 3. some 4. a 5. an 6. some 7. an 8. some 9. a 10. some

Übung 6: 1. men 2. skies 3. children 4. countries 5. women 6. knives 7. feet 8. lives

Übung 7: 1. <u>Where</u> is my cap? 2. <u>Who</u> was angry? 3. <u>What</u> did he give you? 4. <u>When</u> does the exhibition take place? 5. <u>Why</u> is it raining? 6. <u>Where</u> are you going?

Übung 8: 1. took 2. had 3. sang 4. spoke 5. nodded 6. shook 7. gave up 8. was

Übung 9: 1. quietly 2. filthy 3. to shuffle 4. fat 5. reservation 6. to mumble 7. forged

Übung 10: 1. was 2. was 3. was 4. are 5. had been 6. am 7. is 8. will be 9. will be

Übung 11: 1. The government's decision 2. The soldiers' guns 3. The travellers' luggage 4. The President's aeroplane 5. The agent's suggestion 6. The Captain's instructions

Übung 12: 1. The clock had just struck twelve. 2. It was nearly a quarter past five. 3. The men did not know the time. 4. It was very late in the evening. 5. His alarm clock rang at precisely seven o' clock. 6. The old clock was ticking loudly.

Übung 13: 1. was 2. woke up 3. heard 4. knew 5. got 6. threw 7. leapt 8. ran 9. jumped 10. saw 11. thought 12. crept 13. found 14. ran

Übung 14: 1. he was not very happy. 2. what day it was. 3. he needed some evidence 4. Mrs Callaghan said that she was pleased with the results. 5. The thief said that he wanted the money. 6. The teacher said that they were extremely impolite.

Übung 15: narrow, winding, rusty, rickety, old, black, whole, asleep

Übung 16: 1. crowd 2. warship 3. prisoner 4. clue 5. old 6. newspaper 7. breakfast 8. morning. Lösung: children

Übung 17: suddenly, quickly, loudly, violently

Übung 18: 1. An orange is cheaper than a pineapple. 2. The Captain is richer than the cook. 3. A rabbit is faster than a tortoise. 4. A bungalow is lower than a skyscraper. 5. A chair is harder than a sofa.

Übung 19: 1. before 2. before 3. After 4. before 5. after 6. before 7. after

Übung 20: 1. The people were standing in front of the church. 2. He held the child in his arm. 3. The agent looked at the child. 4. The policeman was very angry. 5. The officers were wearing black boots.

Übung 21: 1. painful 2. intelligent 3. happy 4. considerate 5. cheerful 6. important

Übung 22: 1. c 2. a 3. c 4. b 5. c

Übung 23: 1. The suitcase was opened by the agent. 2. The newspaper was read by the man. 3. The orders were shouted by the Captain. 4. The banners were waved by the demonstrators. 5. The taxi was ordered by the tourist. 6. The report was written by the agent.

Übung 24: 1. mine 2. his 3. theirs 4. yours 5. hers 6. ours 7. his 8. ours 9. mine

Übung 25: 1. e 2. g 3. h 4. b 5. a 6. d 7. f 8. c

Übung 26: 1. They're 2. There's 3. He's 4. She's 5. We're

Übung 27: "So, where do you work?" asked his neighbour.

"I work for the city authorities," replied Hunter. This was not the truth, but as a Secret Service man, he had to be careful. You never knew who was a spy.

"Gosh!" replied the man. "That is a coincidence. I work for them too. What Department are you in?"

Hunter told his neighbour that he worked in the Finance Department. Then he turned and went into his flat. He could not face any more awkward questions.

Übung 28: 1. table 2. suitcase 3. wound 4. weak 5. ship

Übung 29: 1. louder 2. better 3. worse 4. more 5. older 6. less

Übung 30: 1. enquired 2. replied 3. reached 4. went 5. took 6. sound 7. hit

Übung 31: 1. over 2. under 3. under 4. over 5. above 6. below

Übung 32: 1. The agent who drives the car is serious. 2. The woman who works in a hospital is a doctor. 3. The nurses who come from Europe are well-trained. 4. The doctors who work long hours are very tired. 5. The receptionist who is writing has brown hair.

Übung 33: 1. b 2. g 3. h 4. e 5. f 6. a 7. c 8. d

Übung 34: 1. Two 2. to 3. to 4. two 5. too 6. too 7. to 8. to 9. too 10. to 11. too

Übung 35: 1. told 2. said 3. heard 4. cried 5. left 6. thought 7. hit 8. dug 9. sang 10. froze

Übung 36: 1. is wearing. 2. is carrying. 3. is whistling. 4. is looking. 5. are working. 6. are repairing. 7. is nearing. 8. are trying

Übung 37: 1. He could see the ship. 2. He could speak Spanish. 3. The soldiers could shoot very well. 4. The Captain can shout extremely loudly. 5. The ship could carry a large amount of ammunition. 6. The torpedo can detonate automatically.

Übung 38: 1. centre 2. information 3. market 4. stomach 5. bakery 6. closed 7. lunchtime 8. because

Übung 39: 1. Who is my neighbour? 2. What is her daughter's name? 3. Where does Rosie live? 4. How are you? 5. How much does the ticket cost? 6. Where are you staying? 7. Whose house is that? 8. Where do the dogs sleep?

Übung 40: 1. and 2. either 3. or 4. Although 5. because 6. both 7. and 8. While

Übung 41: 1. against 2. population 3. voter 4. speech 5. for 6. politician 7. member 8. elect 9. candidate 10. constituency. Lösung: government

Übung 42: 1. Our country does not have its own army. 2. That is not what I think. 3. He was not surprised. 4. I will not give you the details. 5. We do not want any nuclear testing! 6. They would not listen to us.

Übung 43: 1. sadder 2. the saddest 3. sadly 4. sadness 5. more beautiful 6. the most beautiful 7. beautifully 8. beauty

Übung 44: 1. whirred 2. brunette 3. idyllic 4. bamboo 5. stem 6. snatched 7. bandage

Übung 45: 1. her 2. him 3. them 4. us 5. me 6. you 7. it

Übung 46: 1. to defend oneself 2. to hesitate 3. to approach 4. to decide 5. to be located 6. to arm oneself

Übung 47: 1. falsch 2. falsch 3. richtig 4. richtig 5. falsch 6. richtig 7. falsch

Übung 48: "Listen, I've grown fond of you over the last few days."
"Is that supposed to be a declaration of love?"

Übung 49: 1. f 2. c 3. g 4. b 5. d 6. a 7. e

Übung 50: 1. out 2. in 3. in 4. around 5. at 6. between 7. at 8. on

Übung 51: 1. fishermen 2. teeth 3. beaches 4. palm trees 5. berries 6. pairs of shorts

Übung 52: 1. Hunter felt sick and his stomach was sore. 2. There were palm trees along the beach. 3. The leaves of the trees were spiky and green. 4. Their roots were buried in the soil. 5. Waves lapped gently on the sand.

Übung 53: 1. funnel 2. think 3. prior 4. normal 5. manufacture 6. chimney

Übung 54: 1. one half 2. fourteenth 3. two thousand and four 4. one point zero two 5. seven million 6. three quarters 7. zero point two seven

Übung 55: 1. isn't it 2. isn't he 3. haven't they 4. wasn't she 5. weren't we 6. won't they 7. don't I

Übung 56: 1. covered 2. corpse 3. child 4. formed 5. separate 6. through 7. fingers

Übung 57: 1. If we had time, we could find out. 2. If I had more money, I could go on a trip. 3. If she was nice, I would like her.

Übung 58: 1. how 2. when 3. why 4. how 5. when

Übung 59: 1. c 2. a 3. c

Übung 60: 1. pulse 2. scalpel 3. unbearable 4. swarming around 5. examining 6. shade 7. sparsely

Übung 61: tall, neighbouring, thick, dusky, evening, lush, loud, alien, exotic, tropical

Übung 62: 1. unless 2. if/when 3. while 4. and 5. or

Übung 63: 1. The lorry overtook the car. 2. A policeman arrested Hunter. 3. The women picked the oranges. 4. The workers packed the fruit crates. 5. Hunter's colleague gave the instruction.

Übung 64: 1. currency 2. questions 3. disguise 4. radio 5. telephone 6. computer 7. guidebook 8. sunglasses 9. torch. Lösung: equipment

Übung 65: 1. falsch 2. flasch 3. richtig 4. falsch 5. richtig 6. falsch

Übung 66: 1. see 2. have seen 3. saw 4. am seeing 5. had seen 6. will be seeing

Übung 67: 1. The man's sports bag. 2. The country's flag. 3. The country's customs. 4. The tourists' suitcases. 5. The agents' equipment. 6. His colleague's progress.

Übung 68: 1. Headquarters 2. clarification 3. surprised 4. popstar 5. musical 6. entertainment 7. aeroplane

Übung 69: 1. himself 2. themselves 3. ourselves 4. herself 5. yourself 6. itself 7. myself

Übung 70: 1. more thoughtful 2. the most thoughtful 3. thoughtfully 4. thoughtfulness 1. better 2. the best 3. well 4. goodness

Übung 71: 1. His duties. 2. No. 3. Camouflage. 4. No. 5. Quietly. 6. The ship's size, speed and loading capacity.

Übung 72: 1. 1.5 2. 30,000 3. 1984 4. $^5/_8$ 5. 0.54

Übung 73: He prized open the heavy metal door. Behind it there was a long corridor. The agent closed the door and walked forwards. Here it was considerably cooler. There were some wooden boxes with heavy iron hinges. Hunter lifted the lid of one of the boxes. It contained wood-wool. There were machine guns buried in the wool.

Übung 74: 1. f 2. a 3. h 4. i 5. k 6. b 7. j 8. d 9. e 10. g 11. c

Übung 75: 1. nothing 2. no 3. never 4. No one 5. no 6. nowhere

Übung 76: 1. down 2. out 3. in 4. up 5. down 6. in 7. out

Übung 77: 1. could 2. should 3. would 4. could 5. could

Übung 78: 1. Stop fighting! 2. Open the window! 3. Stop now! 4. Evacuate the ship! 5. Start the engine! 6. Leave it there! 7. Help me!

Übung 79: 1. feel 2. tyre 3. murmur 4. weakness 5. blockage 6. happy

Übung 80: 1. They will run a mile tomorrow. 2. You will cycle 20 miles tomorrow. 3. We will/shall play one match tomorrow. 4. He will win three games tomorrow. 5. She will watch five hours of tennis tomorrow.

Übung 81: 1. Ambulances take injured people to hospital. 2. Police cars have blue lights which flash. 3. Fire engines are normally red. 4. Truncheons are weapons carried by policemen. 5. Ambulance drivers receive special training. 6. The sirens make a loud noise.

Übung 82: 1. are getting 2. are talking 3. has 4. is enjoying 5. changes 6. is looking forward 7. is brushing

Übung 83: 1. had had 2. had 3. was having 4. had 5. would have 6. had 7. will have 8. have 9. have 10. will have

Übung 84: 1. drive 2. couple 3. shortly 4. to send 5. to collect 6. junior 7. role 8. current 9. enjoyable

Übung 85: 1. Percy had spoken with Mogudi. 2. The guests had eaten canapés. 3. The security men had checked the invitations. 4. The host had greeted the new arrivals. 5. The woman had taken off their hats and scarves. 6. The men had straightened their ties.

Übung 86: 1. Russian 2. Dutch 3. Swiss 4. Cuban 5. Peruvian 6. Spanish 7. Scottish

Übung 87: you, she, him, he, you, us, you, you, us, it, you

Übung 88: 1. She winks at him. 2. He follows her. 3. The British Ambassador 4. Elegant, rather old-fashioned 5. No

Übung 89: 1. short fat 2. curly grey 3. large handsome 4. small remote tropical 5. new red striped 6. worn leather 7. expensive new 8. cheap second-hand.

Übung 90: 1. work 2. was working 3. worked 4. am working 5. have been working 6. had worked 7. will be working 8. will work/am working 9. am going to work 10. was going to work

Übung 91: 1. became 2. looked 3. left 4. were running 5. were screaming 6. were fired 7. pushed 8. was happening

Übung 92: 1. door 2. ache 3. nervously 4. intelligent 5. socks

Übung 93: 1. In order to help the people, we could give them money. 2. In order to solve the problem, we would have to introduce many measures. 3. In order to contribute to an improvement, the people would have to spend a lot. 4. In order to help him to win, we should cheer him on. 5. In order to secure peace, we would have to put down our weapons.

Übung 94: 1. suddenly 2. sadly 3. diagonally 4. bizarrely 5. presumably 6. briefly 7. simply

Übung 95: 1. interest 2. America 3. population 4. ammunition 5. nuclear 6. accident 7. islands 8. radiation

Übung 96: He said that everything he had done had been for the benefit of his country, even the fact that he had now given the Italians the opportunity to conduct weapons transactions and to launder money in his country.

Übung 97: 1. who 2. whose 3. who 4. that/which 5. whom 6. that/which

Übung 98: 1. Hunter did not see anybody. 2. There was not anything in the boot of the car. 3. He did not have any bullets left. 4. The Governor did not trust anyone. 5. The car did not ever break down. 6. There was not any rust on the bodywork. 7. He did not miss any of his targets.

Übung 99: 1. richtig 2. falsch 3. falsch 4. richtig 5. richtig 6. falsch 7. falsch

Übung 100: 1. up 2. over 3. in 4. up 5. forward 6. up

Übung 101: 1. later 2. the latest 3. lately 4. lateness 1. worse 2. the worst 3. badly 4. badness

Übung 102: 1. I had to do it. 2. We should teach him. 3. She was able to/could see it. 4. They wanted to say it to us. 5. I would have had to do it. 6. We should have taught him. 7. She had been able to see it. 8. They had wanted to say it to us.

Übung 103: 1. a 2. b 3. a 4. c

Übung 104: 1. served 2. sat 3. told 4. saw 5. was 6. hung 7. listened 8. were

Übung 105: 1. He was very tired. 2. The children had to go to bed. 3. The men chatted. 4. There was little evidence. 5. There were many issues to solve. The work would take several months.

Übung 106: 1. target 2. bomb 3. Argentina 4. pistol 5. wreck 6. hazardous 7. explosion 8. bullet 9. success Lösung: torpedoes

Übung 107: 1. f 2. i 3. h 4. b 5. c 6. e 7. d 8. a 9. g

Übung 108: 1. door 2. explained 3. courageous 4. loudly 5. expenses 6. list

Lösungen Abschlusstest

Übung 1: 1. e 2. f 3. a 4. h 5. c 6. g 7. d 8. b
Übung 2: 1. him 2. us 3. she 4. we 5. I 6. she 7. He 8. we
Übung 3: 1. but 2. and 3. Because 4. Although 5. until 6. either or
Übung 4: 1. to 2. up 3. out 4. off 5. for 6. out 7. into/onto 8. through 9. over 10. at
Übung 5: 1. expensive 2. difficult 3. enthusiastic 4. friendly 5. flickering
Übung 6: 1. islands 2. weapons 3. vehicle 4. luggage 5. fruits 6. nationalities 7. body
Übung 7: 1. slow 2. bright 3. energetic 4. discontented 5. poor
Übung 8: "Where are you going?" asked the lorry driver.
"I'm going back to my hotel," said Hunter.
At 10.00 p.m., they arrived at the hotel.
"Gosh!" exclaimed the driver. "Is that where you're staying?"
Hunter replied that the hotel had been allocated by the Secret Service.
Übung 9: 1. There is no one there! 2. We have not been to the beach! 3. They could not have seen the explosion. 4. You are going to find out soon! 5. I have wanted to visit that island!
Übung 10: 1. sad 2. angry 3. relevant 4. healthy 5. hot 6. warm 7. able 8. powerful
Übung 11: 1. to speak 2. to shake 3. to fall 4. to sink 5. to say 6. to begin 7. to hold 8. to pay 9. to tell 10. to get 11. to become 12. to find 13. to think